ODDBALL THOUGHTS

ODDBALL THOUGHTS

DONALD SILVERMAN

Copyright © 2024 Donald Silverman
All rights reserved, including the right of reproduction in whole or in part in any form without the express written permission of the publisher.

Printed in the United States of America

The characters and events portrayed in this book are stylized. Any similarity to real persons, living or dead, is coincidental and not intended by the author.

No part of this book may be reproduced, or stored in a retrieval system, or transmitted in any form or by any means, electronic, mechanical, photocopying, recording, or otherwise, without express written permission of the publisher.

ISBN-13: 978-1-0882-8691-3

Cover design by: "Mad Dog" AKA Barry Gottlieb & Erik Goyenechea
Library of Congress Control Number: 2018675309
Printed in the United States of America

theothersilverman.com

This book is dedicated to my dear wife Mary Anne for tolerating my weird point of view, and for her excellent editing skills. And to my sons, Daniel and Corey, for tolerating my nonsense for so many years. And to "Mad Dog," AKA Barry Gottlieb, for helping me structure and organize my essays.

Also, to Susan Berkowitz, for bringing out the writer who was hiding inside my brain. For my friends Steve Greenberg and Stan Gedzelman, for encouraging my weird sense of humor. And to my friends in the Sun Valley East (Boynton Beach, FL) Writer's Group for continuing to laugh.

CONTENTS

Dedication   v
Foreword   xiii

101 DONALD SILVERMANS   1

LOOSE ENDS   5

MY OOMPH   9

NOTHING   11

LOST   13

SUNSET BOULEVARD   15

49TH ANNIVERSARY   17

MOMISMS   19

THE BARNETT FAMILY   21

MONTREAL CEMETERY   25

WHAT'S LIFE WORTH?   27

WHY   29

I DON'T UNDERSTAND   31

I HAD A DREAM	33
I NEVER THOUGHT I'D LIVE TO SEE THE END OF THE WORLD	37
HIDING IN PLAIN SIGHT	39
PERFECT WORLD	41
HERE'S WHAT I DON'T WANT TO BE	43
I SHOULDA COULDA WOULDA	45
I WANT TO	49
I'VE HAD ENOUGH VIRUS TALK	51
ANYTHING CAN BE	55
ALL OF MY FAMILY ARE WEIRDOS AND ALL OF MY FRIENDS ARE QUIRKY	59
EVERY SHIRT HAS A STAIN AND STORY TO GO WITH IT	63
MY REFRIGERATOR	65
FASCINATION	67
GREAT MINDS	69
CLICHÉ LOVE	73
HENRY HUDSON PARK	77
CROSSING PATHS	81
TECHNOLOGY	83
THE COMMUNE	85

BAD HABITS	89
MY GOOD FRIEND NEIL	93
SIMCA	95
THE NOISE	97
US POSTAL SERVICE CHANGE OF ADDRESS FORM	101
TOO MUCH, TOO LITTLE, TOO EXPENSIVE	105
COSTCO	109
SEPHARDIC WEDDING	111
I USED TO	113
AN IMPRECISE GUY LIVING IN A PRECISE WORLD	115
WELLCARE	119
SMOKING POT	123
TRUST	127
WHAT'S IN A NAME?	131
SILVERMAN PRODUCTIONS	133
IF I COULD FLY	135
THE SMALL PRINT	137
BIGGER, BIGGER, BIG TUSH LOTTERY	139
ARM SEX	143

CONTENTS

MEATBALL WAR	145
SOUTHBOUND SUBWAY	147
A MOMENT IN TIME	149
49 YEARS LATER AND HERE WE ARE IN SUN VALLEY EAST	153
ALL OF MY FRIENDS ARE QUIRKY	155
AN OLD FART'S GUIDE TO PLANET EARTH	159
ROCKAWAY PLAYLAND	161
THE TOOTH FAIRY	165
ROUND THINGS	167
PUBLIC RESTROOM REPORT	169
MAILBOX	173
MASKED	175
MY PHONE IS BROKEN, MY SHOES DON'T FIT, AND I'M NOT WEARING A BRA ANYMORE	177
MYSTERIES OF THE UNIVERSE	179
NEW AND IMPROVED	183
NOAH ZARK	187
STORAGE	191
VISITING DOCTORS	193
31 YEARS IN THE FILM BUSINESS	195

IS THAT ALL THERE IS?	197
IT'S ALL GONE	201
JUST YESTERDAY	203
KUKULITZ	205
THE ME NOBODY KNOWS	209

FOREWORD

Discovering your inner self is a strange exercise. You think you know who you are from an early age. You go to school and take tests. You meet with a Guidance Counselor and she makes an assessment. Your parents and their friends develop some opinions about what they think are your strengths. (Hey, he's tall. Let's aim him towards a school that has a good basketball team.)

Yet somewhere deep down inside there is the real you. But you're not quite sure how to unlock him.

About four years ago a neighbor invited me to join a writer's group.. My knee-jerk response was: "I'm not a writer."

Her reply: "Sure you are. I've seen your emails."

Well, I reluctantly agreed to join the group for one session. And yes, I would write a short essay to read to them.

And so I did. I can't remember what I wrote about. But I do remember that they laughed. And that was all I needed to convince me that I could be a writer.

Four years later, I'm still writing. And they're still laughing.

Oddball Thoughts are a series of short essays that explore the meandering mind of Donald Silverman. The offbeat, fresh, perspective topics are quirky, funny, persnickety, silly and strange. If you enjoy probing the off eat side of everyday life, then Oddball Thoughts is right up your alley. Read more at theothersilverman.com.

Thanks for reading my nonsense.

-Donald Silverman
April, 2024

Oddball Thoughts

101 Donald Silvermans

"Honey, it's time."

"I know, I know, I'm just finishing up a great dream."

"Can you finish it on the plane? We're heading to JFK and we don't know where to park the car."

"I'll be up in a minute".

TV speaker: "... recently reported that working nights can cause cancer. But first, this is Today on NBC.."

"Did you hear that?"

"What?"

"They said that working nights can cause cancer."

"Yeah, and so does MSG, passive smoke and body odor."

"Honey, did you pack your meds?"

"Yeah."

"Do you have a plastic bag for my shaver and stuff?"

"It's in the kitchen to the left of the sink."

"Do you want to take anything to read on the plane?"

"I'll pick up the New York Times at the airport."

"Did you pack your computer?"

"Got it."

It's 6:00 AM in Brooklyn Heights. We head out of our apartment building and pass a local food cart merchant talking to a friend who owns a taxicab.

"Need a ride, lady.?"

"No thanks, we're fine."

"It's so quiet out here."

"You'd be amazed how busy the subways are at 6 AM. Jam packed. Especially the #s 2 & 4 heading into the city."

The car is parked just beyond a dumpster, a block from our apartment.

"Great spot."

"Yeah, I got lucky."

We load our bags and head down Montague Street passing a myriad of ethnic restaurants, real estate offices, banks, an eyeglass store and who-knows-what as we zoom off to the Atlantic Avenue entrance to the BQE.

The ride to JFK is uneventful. Well, except for the fact that my mind went into automatic pilot and we ended up crossing the Verrazano Bridge heading towards Staten Island.

"HONEY! Did you plan to visit Staten Island on the way to the airport?"

"Oh, shit. I can't believe I did this. I'll bet the asshole toll collector will charge me nine bucks just to turn around."

"Well, at least there's no traffic heading back."

We managed to find the long-term parking lot without any problem, hopped on the free shuttle to Delta and made a beeline for the departures desk.

"Can I see your ID?" No greeting, no smile. But, hey, it's New York. The parade of people to her slot at the terminal must be mind numbing.

"Anything else?"

"We couldn't find our Delta SkyMiles cards, can you check your computer to see if we're in there somewhere? It shouldn't be too hard to find Donald Silverman."

"Mister, there are 101 Donald Silvermans in our computer." 101 Donald Silvermans? Get your hands around that one at 7 AM in the morning.

I didn't think much about that until I got on the plane. And, then I started to wonder, what could it be like to be another Donald

Silverman? I guess I'd have to make a few assumptions: most of us were probably born in New York or Chicago. Most grew up in a middle class home (just because it's a middle of the road kind of name). More are likely to have a postgraduate degree (my son, the doctor/lawyer). And, most grew up in a Jewish home.

Or am I just projecting an image of what I think Donald Silverman should be?

This could be an interesting project. It just might be a real eye-opener. After all, we all have pre-conceived notions of who we are and how we think others see us. Maybe there's a Donald Silverman who is a Presbyterian Minister in Leavenworth, Kansas? Or, a Donald Silverman who travels the world jumping from one cargo ship to another. Maybe there's a Donald Silverman who owns a steamship company in Kuala Lumpur? And, maybe I'm heading back into my morning dream?

I could start this research on the web by searching for Donald Silverman and see what comes up. But, that would only give me part of the picture. What about the Donald Silvermans who are just everyday schmoes? Or older Donald Silvermans who missed the Cyber Age and are happy just to lay back, relaxing after a hard career driving a school bus.

Maybe Delta Airlines would let me get into their computer and I could canvas all of the others with my name. Then I could ask them what it's like to be another Donald Silverman. Are they happy? Is their life lucky? Was their mother neurotic? Do they have a crazy extended family? Or are they just a cross section of schmoes with the same name?

Then again, maybe I'm thinking too much. Maybe it's just like that Zen saying: "it is what it is, and there ain't no is-er." Maybe I just got lucky that the ticket agent found the one Donald Silverman that I needed her to find so I could get a few points on my *SkyMiles* account. I wonder if the other Donald Silvermans forget their number.

And I wonder if they wonder about the rest of us.

Loose Ends

"Anyone who really gets to know me either falls in love with me or ends up wanting to murder me. Sometimes both."

ANONYMOUS

While my life has not exactly been a series of loose ends, it could be considered a contender. When I was a kid I wasn't interested in hearing or reading stories from end-to-end. If I jumped into the middle and exited about two-thirds of the way down, I felt like I got the gist of it and that seemed to satisfy my curiosity.

"But, what about the end? Don't you want to know about how it ended?" Not really. I could easily make up my own ending and be perfectly satisfied. Maybe it was because I never liked sad endings. Or maybe it was because it was more fun to make up my own ending. Or maybe I had Attention Deficit Disorder but they didn't diagnose this sort of malady back in the day.

Although I have to admit that sometimes the ending of a story was pretty good. I remember I had a friend who wanted to be a disc jockey at a radio station. His name was something like Mike Sheckenhopper. It didn't exactly roll off one's tongue. One day he was at his girlfriend's house and her parents weren't home. As you would expect, they were playing around. The TV was on. The movie *South Pacific* was just ending. The announcer mentioned one of the star's names—"Starring Gordon McCrae." At that moment his girlfriend jumped up from the couch, flying in the air in her birthday suit when she yelled, "Mike McCay, there's your radio name, Mike McCay!". Five seconds later, her parents returned and opened the door. A missed opportunity to tie up their loose ends, so to speak.

So I just meandered along through playground games, classrooms, and work just sort of diving into and exiting out of situations whenever it seemed to suit me.

I remember playing softball in the street outside of my house in Long Beach, New York. We lived near the end of the boulevard, so there wasn't ever much traffic. Sometimes I started to play when the game began. Other times I just jumped in. The game didn't mean much to me. Who won? Who lost? Who cared? But, one time we took a break and the conversation turned to sex. I was about 11 or 12 years old then, so my ears perked up pretty fast. I remember there was some discussion about the mechanics of sex. The guy does this, the girl does that. They huff and puff and they smoke a cigarette. I don't recall how they started but I do recall how it ended. Afterwards I thought, well, someday I'll learn about how to get this boy/girl thing rolling so I can tie up the loose end.

Even from the beginning, school was a blur to me. You read a story and then the teacher wanted to know what you learned. I got bored pretty fast so there wasn't much to report. Occasionally I read the Cliff Notes. I knew that Jack and Jill ran up the hill but I never really knew why, when, or where it occurred.

Somehow, I passed high school, undergraduate school, and even graduate school. To be honest, I think the teachers just wanted to push me through the system rather than helping me figure out where and why I fell off the wagon. I always knew enough information to make it through the tests, and even better through the essays. I guess I finally realized that I wanted to tell stories because I wanted to make up my own beginnings and endings.

So here I am telling lots of stories. I live a disjointed life. I jump from one thing to another. No beginnings or endings. I just go for a laugh.

"I was gonna take over the world this morning but I overslept. Postponed. Again."

Anonymous

My Oomph

I used to have a lot of oomph. I think most of us had it when we were young. You woke up and got out of bed. Then you were off to the races. Brush your teeth, get dressed, tie your shoes, chow down breakfast and go to school. Recess came and you flew out the classroom door and ran out to the playground. Your feet flew into the air and you ran and ran and ran until time was up and you needed to return to your class.

If there was snow outside you ran home, put on your winter coat and your boots, grabbed your sled, and off you went to the big hill across the street. You ran up that hill like it was nothing, just nothing...and sleighed down as fast as you could. You did it again and again and again and again. Not once did you stop to think if you were tired or out of energy, or if another ride was worth the effort.

I used to conquer the stairs in our apartment building with the same gusto. We lived on the sixth floor. When it was time to go out I ran to the staircase and leaped six or eight stairs at a time. Two or three leaps and one staircase was done. And then, onto the next one. More leaps. Dong...dong...dong. Did I ever think I would hurt myself? Or break a bone? Nah. That thought never crossed my mind. The game was all about how fast I could leap down six flights of stairs. It was a game between me and me and it was a ton of fun.

Other times, I would get into a snowball fight. It would just start innocently. One kid would throw a snowball. The other kid would return the throw. Before you knew it it was a war that went on for what seemed like forever. Did we stop to eat lunch? No. Did we stop for a drink? No. We just continued to war until our hands were so cold we couldn't feel our fingers.

And then the years just passed us by. We were 20 and 40 and 60 and we hit our mid-70s. We still played some physical games. We ran and swam and knocked a ball around on a court. Until... the oomph hit some of us. Getting up in the morning was an *oy*. Tying your shoes was an *ay ay*. Taking a walk was okay until you realized you needed to walk back home.

Didn't they sell a product in the 1960s called Geritol? It was supposed to treat "tired blood". "Just two tablespoons would provide you with the iron of two pounds of calves liver."

Oh, what an image that was.

And, didn't they sell Brylcreem? A product that would give life to your dry hair.

"A little dab will do you."

While it didn't actually give you oomph, It was more of a psychological boost to your tired life.

So, now we're in the gilded years. My mother used to call them the *"OY"* years. Everything hurts. Everything is an effort. Getting into forward motion is a bit like moving a locomotive. It's a slow push, mostly uphill to get the ball rolling. Then all is good until you stop for a breather.

Maybe you sit on a bench for a while and take in the fresh air. It's usually a nice reprieve from the walk. Until. .. you need to get the locomotive back into gear.

Maybe some Brylcreem isn't such a bad idea. What would be wrong with a little dab that will do ya?

Nothing

(Long Pause)
"What are you doing?"
"Nothing"
"What's nothing?"
"It's the opposite of something."
"How do you do nothing?"
"I dunno."
"It's a time/space sort of thing."
"Really?"
"Yeah."
"Well, how do you do it?"
"I'm not entirely sure but, I can tell you this...I'm an expert at it."
"Really?"
"Yeah. I can sit in front of a TV and see and hear nothing. I'm actually an expert at this. Sometimes you just need to lay in your bed and do nothing for three years."

I think I discovered at an early age that most things that people think are something are really nothing. So, I learned to focus on nothing, And, you know what? ... I'm really happy doing nothing. Because .. you don't have to repeat what's on the news, what the movie was about, what you had for dinner last night, what was on the shopping list...

Doing nothing is really akin to defocusing. It's like wearing an out-of-focus pair of glasses and not being bothered to get a new prescription.

"Nothing" is probably a learned behavior. My Dad was a Nothing Expert. He worked hard. He came home, ate dinner, and did nothing. And he was happy as a clam.

"I am busy doing nothing… that the idea of doing anything – which as you know, always leads to something– cuts into the nothing and then forces me to have to drop everything."

JERRY SEINFELD

"In my house there's this light switch that doesn't do anything. Every so often I would flick it on and off just to check it. Yesterday, I got a call from a woman from Madagascar. She said, "Cut it out."

STEVEN WRIGHT

So, what do you do when you finish doing nothing? I take a nap.

I don't know if I shed any light on doing nothing but I'll leave you with this Groucho quote: "Time flies like an arrow. Fruit flies like a banana."

Now there's nothing to think about the next time you're doing nothing.

Lost

I'm looking for a joke. Not any joke but the best joke I've ever heard. It was the kind of joke that hit my funny bone really, really hard. The first time I heard it, I couldn't stop laughing. The more I heard it, the more I laughed. It just might have been the funniest joke I ever heard. It's the kind of joke you read on the internet and you burst out laughing all by yourself. That's the best kind of joke, because you don't have to run it up the politically correct ladder to see if it's okay to share with anybody.

But there's a problem with this joke. I lost it. I can't remember the joke to save my life. How is this possible? How can you forget something that had such a visceral impact on your day...your week...your year? I'm sure I told this joke to 50 people. As I recall, all of them laughed. Considering I have a wide range of friends and relatives who have an internal mechanism to field their ability to laugh at a joke, this joke surely was a joke for all ages.

What's a fella to do when he can't find what he lost? He asks his family and old friends,"do you remember that really funny joke I told you 25+ years ago? You know, the one that made milk come out of your nose. We both fell on the floor laughing. Oh, come on, you can remember it.."

Okay, fair enough. I did share many jokes with you over the years. Some were funny, others were kind of funny and some were groaners...but, usually good groaners.

Maybe I should go on the internet and look up, "what's the funniest joke ever?" What do you think the odds are of finding my favorite joke?

Slim to none. It's not because my joke was the funniest ever. It's because my joke was the funniest ever to me. It hit my funny bone.

I remember watching or hearing an interview with a comedian who was not well known. The interviewer asked him, "how do you know when a joke is funny?"

Without batting an eye he responded, "If I think it's funny, it's funny."

How could I finish this ditty without telling a joke? Now, this isn't *the* joke but, the first time I heard it I thought it was pretty funny. Warning: It's definitely not PC.

A bear walks into a bar. Slams down his paw on the bar and says to the bartender, "Give me a beer."

The bartender looks at the bear and simply states, "We don't serve beer to bears."

The bear is a bit perturbed. He taps his paw on the bar again and says, "Give me a beer."

The bartender responds without even looking up, "We don't serve beer to bears in our bar in Bellingham."

The bear is now getting a bit pissed off. This time he slams his paw on the bar and says, "Now, give me a damn beer or .. you see that woman at the end of the bar? If you don't give me a beer I'm going to eat that woman."

And then he proceeds to walk to the end of the bar and in "poof" the woman disappears. The bartender looks at the bear very carefully and says, "Let me say this one more time. We don't serve beer to bears in our bar in Bellingham who do drugs."

The bear looks at him with a quizzical look. "You don't serve beer to bears in your bar in Bellingham who do drugs?"

The bartender paused to smile and said, "It's about that bar-bitch you ate."

Sunset Boulevard

It was 1969. I was 22 years old. I had finished my Army tour of duty six months beforehand. Somehow I fell into a small business opportunity sharing the ownership of a retail lighting store. My high school friend's father owned a wholesale electronics store in NYC. He agreed to provide us with inventory on consignment. While neither one of us was remotely experienced or capable of operating a store we were pretty good at attracting young women.

One of the items we sold in the store was a blinking light box that responded to the beat of pulsating music. The local Long Island night clubs were attracted to this point of sale concept.

To make a long story short, a women's wear dress manufacturer stopped in and liked the light box concept. He asked us to come out to Los Angeles to set up a prototype. So, two starstruck kids closed up the store and made a beeline hike to LA.

It didn't take long for the deal to fall through. Too many promises on a wish and a prayer. I took a job parking cars at a very upscale restaurant. My partner flew back to NY for his Grandfather's funeral.

The first weekend arrived and I was all alone. What's a boy to do? Maybe I'll just walk up to the corner of Sunset Blvd. and hitchhike to the Beverly Hills beach.

Along comes a big 1960s Chevy Convertible with NY license plates. A British guy was in the driver's seat. He looked at me and said, "Where are you heading?" I said I was heading to the beach. He said, "Hop in."

So, off we went along Sunset Boulevard heading to the beach in Beverly Hills. Two strangers. No apparent plans. As the car cruised along, so did the conversation. "Where are you from? What do you do? Why are you here?" Etc. Etc.

While I'm not sure how long it took to get to the beach, the conversation flowed pretty comfortably. Turns out, neither one of us had a plan for the day. Although I did have a fantasy to find the actress Carol Lindley somewhere on the beach , A boy's dream. Hey, that never happened. Oh, well. At least I had a goal for the day.

As I recall, we spent a lovely afternoon chatting about this and that. And then, as the day came to an end, we hopped back into the Chevy and headed back along Sunset Boulevard.

Somewhere along the way I learned that my new friend was recently divorced, he was working as an accountant for one of the movie studios. He just moved to LA. He didn't know a soul.

I was his first point of contact, Well, we arrived back to the original street corner, traded phone numbers and parted ways. A week went by and he called me. Want to go out for dinner? Sure, but I don't have any money. No worries, I'll be glad to treat. Well, the dinner was lovely. We talked more about this and that. It ended, We parted ways.

Another dinner followed a week later. More congenial conversation.

And then, I moved to San Francisco. We never communicated again. No calls. No letters. No goodbyes.

The late 1960s were an innocent time. We didn't fear meeting strangers. We didn't expect strange or dangerous things to happen. Or, maybe it was just a few like me? I still cherish the memory.

49th Anniversary

I was 21. Footloose and fancy free. I got my DD214 (Honorable Discharge from the US Army) and I was back to part-time college at Nassau Community College.

I had an old friend who invited me to share his artist's loft above a movie theatre. He was subletting for some guy I never met. It was cheap (about $85 a month each). This was a really unusual space. The ceiling was easily 18 feet tall. There was a bathroom and a kitchen (which we never used because of the rodent situation, but who cared? We didn't bother them and they didn't bother us. There was a stairway that divided the loft space and reached up to two opposing lofts. There was a decent diner downstairs where you could get a good tuna on toasted rye with french fries for under 5 bucks.

I had a car and a stupid daytime job working for an insurance investigation company. I drove to school a few days a week.

Nassau Community College was a commuter college. Nobody lived on campus. If you wanted to make friends, you needed to hang out in the student lounge between classes.

Now, here I was a 6'2" skinny (yeah, I was once skinny) part-time college kid who had curly hair down to his shoulders and a big bushy blonde-ish beard. I was wearing my favorite red, white and blue striped jeans and, I'm sure, a completely non-matching shirt. Not exactly the fella your parents would want your daughter to meet at college.

On one not so particular day, I was just hanging out there talking with my friends about nothing in particular. A cute girl walks in. I'm sure I glanced at her and she glanced at me. But that was about it. *UNTIL*, she approached me and started some small talk. Being a very shy fellow, I was enamored with the idea of being "picked up." I dunno. We talked for 10, 20 or 30 minutes, and then it was time for me to head to my geology class. I asked her if she would like to come. She declined. Then I told her I had to go and said goodbye.

It was a cold night on campus. The buildings were spread out like it was designed as a WWII airport (which it originally was). I didn't ask for her phone number and so I figured that was that. But alas...that was not the case. Apparently she asked her friends in the student lounge if it would seem too forward to wait for me after my class got out. (How she knew where my class was occuring is still amazing to me). In any case, the class ended. I walked out of the building and there she was. Holy cow! This kind of thing never happened to me. I thought it was a movie scene.

The rest of the story is pretty predictable. We dated. We moved in together. We moved to a friend's hippy commune for a while. She got her first job as a nurse at a Manhattan hospital. I won a few big Off-Track Betting bets. She was amazed. Of course, I gave back the winnings over the next year of betting. We first moved in with two of her nurse friends. Tight quarters. So we moved into our own apartment. Then we moved to Staten Island–where I went to college. Two kids came along.

Off to Richmond, VA for 31 years. Back to NYC. Four grandkids came along. And now we're soon to celebrate our 49th Anniversary.

Miracles happen.

Momisms

In the 1950s just about every mother had a bag of expressions that she used on a daily basis. I'm guessing they were timetested word groups drawn from the family lexicon. Every time you heard one "if I told you once I told you a million times..." it still had meaning (well, some meaning anyway). My mother's expressions were Yiddish mixed with English–kind of a Pig Latin. It was a sort of shorthand. Instead of having to explain why you should leave her alone, her expression simply got right to the point, *"Gay kaken ofn yahm!"* (Go shit in the ocean or, Go jump in the lake.)

She was never a big fan of hearing a *spiel* (long, involved sales pitch).

My mother also wasn't any different than any other Jewish mother of her time. And as kids were apt to do, we continued to ask questions upon questions as my mother would pull out her standard line: "Stop hocking me a *chainik*" (quit bothering her).

She also had a great repertoire of "f-words" in sentences. No, not that one. Words like *farblondjet* (I can't find what I was just doing), *ferkakte* (crazy or messed up...it's really a clean word but it sounds a little dicey), *farshtunken* ("It doesn't work because it's a *farshtunkene* machine").

"That *furshlugginer* girl got pregnant, and her *farkakte* parents kicked her out."

Another classic was her use of the word *ungapatchka* (tacky, ostentatious, ridiculously overdone or tasteless). "Don't go outside wearing that outfit. It's *ungapatchka*."

She often called me a *pischer*, *noodnik* and a pain in the *kishke*. And, if I was bad I got a *"patsh* in the *tookus."*

If she didn't trust someone she called them a *shmegegge* – someone who was full of baloney, hot air; nonsense. She loved to refer to men who were bald as "*tuchus kups* (ass heads). "Leo, would you look at that *tuchus kup*?"

On the bright side, my mother always liked to *shmooze* (small talk). And on occasion, "'*plotz* with joy" (at a graduation or bar mitzvah). But always preceded with a *kinehora* (sending evil spirits away), and *sei gesund* was often said as a feeling of good wishes (Be well).

My mother actually had quite an array of great Yiddish words she used frequently: *kibbitz* (joke around), *tuchus, tooshie, schlock* (cheap or shoddy material), *bupkis* (nothingness), *chazerei* (junk, trash, anything disgusting), *mishegas* (craziness, a teenager stealing his parents' car), *megillah* (a long involved story), *schmooze, oy gevalt* (oh my), *oy vey* (oh my) , *vey is mir, guttenyu* (Oh God, woe is me)—these foreign phonemes were the music of my childhood as much as the songs of the Andrews Sisters and The Pretenders.

In the end, she always wished someone "*A bi gezunt*," (as long as you're healthy), implying "nothing else matters."

CREDITS TO: MY YIDDISHE MOMMA TOLD ME...AND OTHER YIDDISH EXPRESSIONS–WHAT A LANGUAGE! AUTHOR UNKNOWN

The Barnett Family

My mother was one of eight Barnett kids. Half were born in Russia and the other half in New York City. Half had deep European accents that you could cut with a knife. The others sounded like the deep Bronx. I never knew anything about my Grandfather. With 10 mouths to feed, I'm guessing he was a hard working guy. Probably in the garment industry. Apparently, my grandmother was a little confused when my mother was born. She named her Sarah but called her Sadie. My mother hated that name so she, in turn, called herself Shirley. Anyway, I never got the whole story on this identity crisis. Shirley was Shirley and that was that.

My mother was the baby. While I never met my Uncle George (I think he died in one of the wars), the rest of them were really characters. Nathan was the oldest. He lived in the Bronx. I have no idea what he did for a living but when he got into his 80s, I was told he "played the horses." I was told he went to the racetrack several days a week. And somehow he figured out a way to handicap the winners. Did he only report his winnings? Who knows? Many years later, I was told that Nathan refused to come to my wedding because I married a *shiksa*. Did I miss him? No, not really.

Howard ran an illegal poker and betting parlor in Montreal. He was a bachelor. Always dressed to the nines. Three-piece suits that were custom made to fit around his ample belly. He lived in the Mount Royal Hotel. Room service, maid service...you need it, you got it. We met him once a year in New York City. He took us all out for lunch at the Stage Deli. Mile high pastrami sandwiches with rich, thick deli mustard and a good sour pickle. When the check came, he reached into his pocket and dug out a huge wad of cash. I never saw so much money in my whole life. Uncle Howard was a happy guy. Sadly, he died broke.

Jack was a happy go lucky tombstone salesman. He was married to Esther. No kids. For some odd reason, Aunt Esther smoked like a chimney and chewed on her tongue. I have no idea why she chewed on her tongue. But, since I chew on my fingers (oral fixation, I guess), her tongue chewing didn't bother me.

Jack was a born salesman.

He had the gift of gab and a tremendous sense of humor. One time a customer visited him at work. After a bit of kibitzing, he asked the woman what she wanted to have inscribed on her husband's tombstone. Without hesitating she replied, "Rest in pieces." He laughed. She didn't.

Another time he came to our house in Long Beach (after a long drive from Montreal). He rang the doorbell, headed right for the bathroom, flushed the toilet and came out to announce, "Good, it works." He laughed. So did we.

Rae was one of my mother's sisters. She lived with Sam Mouckley and their son, Mike Mouckley, in an apartment in Montreal (his name always sounded like a bookie to me). Rae was a housewife and Sam was a barber. They came to visit us in NYC in the late 1950s. Sam was amazed to see so many pizza signs. He announced, "Pizza, Pizza, Pizza .. What's Pizza?" He was simply flabbergasted. A few years later my mother said, "We should open up a pizza store." Too bad we didn't. It was and is a good business. One time, when I was about 6 or 7 years old I was in my Aunt Rae's kitchen. She was making *kishka* (stuffed derma). And, while she was stuffing it, air got caught in the casing and it sounded like a big fart. Well I almost died laughing, and I guess my laugh was contagious because my aunt couldn't stop laughing either. It was a wonderful moment.

Anna was my mother's oldest sister. Since there were 8 kids in the family and she was the oldest, I'm guessing she was about 25 years older. My mother always told me she was a "surprise." Anna and her husband Morris lived in The Bronx in a 5-story walk up. Morris was a skinny fellow and Anna was "ample." How she managed to negotiate those stairs with groceries was a near miracle. My mother and Anna spoke often on the phone. Anna had a thick European accent. Their conversations often sounded like Yiddish Pig Latin. "So, vats doing? De kinter okay? Vat so you vant me to bring mits Peseah?"

"Oy, you could brrring tsmis mit plenty prunes. It voiks good, ya know."

Morris would always conduct the Passover seder from cover-to-cover in Hebrew. Three hours minimum. About 10 minutes into the reading my sister and I would go into their bedroom. She was about 11 and I was about 6. She would start to wardrobe me in Aunt Anna's clothing and jewelry...pearls and lipstick and all kinds of paraphernalia. And of course, her makeup. Lots of it. Then the show would begin. My sister paraded me around the table. The somber mood quickly turned to laughter. Even Uncle Morris cracked up. It was a moment in family history to behold.

Dave was the closest in age to my mother. He was married to Bess. I think he was an accountant or bookkeeper for a department store in Montreal. Good solid guy who played by the rules of life. Honest, loving and reliable. Bess was a housewife who spoke French and English. She once shared this practical wisdom with her young nephew: "Donald, do you know the difference between a man and a woman? Plumbing."

I was only about 10 when she told this to me. So you can imagine it took me a few years to understand the depth of this concept.

And, then I thought, "well, maybe plumbing was not such a bad career choice?"

Montreal Cemetery

My mother was one of eight. That was a blessing and a curse. Sadly, she had to witness all of their deaths before hers. The next to last to pass was Dave. My 82-year old mother and her 75-year old nephew Seymour wanted to attend the funeral. So did my sister. For some weird reason we flew from Kennedy Airport on LAN Chile Airlines. I think we caught it on a stop over from Santiago to Montreal. As I remember it was a beautiful plane with great food. I don't remember much about my uncle's funeral, but I do remember a follow up event. My mother wanted to visit the graves of her parents. My aunt's nephew told us which cemetery to visit and approximately where the graves were located. It was a chilly and windy day. We drove into the cemetery and I volunteered to look for the headstones. I walked one aisle and the next. I walked another and the next. By the third aisle, I started walking backwards to avoid the cold wind. All of a sudden some pollen must have tickled my nose. My eyes closed and I blasted out a huge sneeze. I opened my eyes and I was standing in front of my Uncle Jack's headstone (remember he was the funny uncle who flushed the toilet when he came to visit us). I was sure Jack was saying, "Hey schmuck, I'm right here."

I was standing in the middle of this Jewish cemetery laughing. Then I walked back to the car where my mother and sister were waiting. I told them the story. We all had a hardy laugh. Jack would have loved to see this visceral response. I never did find my grandparent's headstones. But, I'm guessing they too, would have had a great laugh.

What's Life Worth?

Back in the day, when I produced TV spots and public relations videos, I was hired to create a video for the American Heart Association. They wanted to send out a message to the public about the various types of heart disease and the success modern medicine had using new medicine and treatments.

They gathered a group of people who they knew had some kind of a success story. Now, when you're conducting interviews with what we in the production business called, "real people" it's easy to get the facts. But if you're looking for more depth, you need to ask just the right question.

After about ten pretty ordinary interviews about stroke, heart attacks, coronary disease, etc., I interviewed an attorney who had received a heart transplant. I went through the obvious questions about how his heart disease was discovered, how it progressed, and how he discovered that he needed a heart transplant. I thought this guy must have more to say (remember, he's a lawyer and they like to wax poetic). So, I paused for a moment and said, "What's life worth?"

His reply: "What's life worth? *Hmm*...well, let's see. Last year I attended my daughter's college graduation. This year I attended my son's law school graduation. My son and his wife brought me a grandson about two weeks ago. You tell me what life's worth."

When I decided to circulate this prompt my wife asked me the same question, "What's life worth?" I thought for a moment and then said, "Well, it's about love, it's about caring, it's about hearing the birds in the morning and smooching with your puppy, it's about watching a movie that makes you cry...it's about creating something and discovering something. It's about attraction, affection, aggravation and copulation. It's about hearing your 3-year-old Grandson tell you that you're funny.

I attended a Zoom funeral yesterday for an old friend. We knew each other for 50 years. Holy cow! We met by chance on a beach. He was with his friends and they were looking for a place to drop their blanket. I told him this is as good a place as any. We started to talk and talk and talk and laugh and laugh. Clearly, we had a strong sense of silliness in common. We both grew up in Jewish homes and attended Hebrew School. They taught us lots of words and songs and traditions. At that age, it didn't seem to add up to a can of beans. But, somehow we stored all of that mumbo jumbo and turned it into our own secret language. Much of it is boyhood bathroom humor. But, oh did we laugh…like little boys are apt to do.

What's life worth? Ten minutes of silliness with Jeff would make my day. He knew just how to hit my funny bone. Guys like Jeff don't just fall off a tree everyday. I'll miss you Jeff. And, I hope you find some other silly guys on your new journey.

Why

Why does a toilet need a seat? Why does a bureau need a knob? Why does a knob need a screw? And who knows what goes on in that room after the lights go out? A screw...a washer and...oh my...

Why do birds need bees? And, why do bees need seeds?

It seems as if Noah...remember that Ark guy...was right: "It takes two to tango."

Why does a chair have a seat? And a lamp have a switch? A floor have a groove? Why must a wheel be round? And why must gravity always pull you down?

I'd like to know. I'd like to know. I'd like to know. I'd really like to know...

And who became the decider? Someone...something...somehow...

We had a decider a few years back. But, nobody believed him.

There were a lot of decisions to make.

Why does a chair or a table need legs? Where are they going? And, why do my legs need pants?

Why does lotion need motion? Isn't motion just meant for the ocean? Yet, a pond just sits still.

Why does a washer need a dryer? Why does an iron need a board?

Why does a teacher need a student? And, why does a student need homework? Now, we're getting to the heart of it.

It's all about why. Not where. Not when. Not how. But, why? Why can't you stop asking these stupid questions?

I Don't Understand

I don't understand guilt. Never did. Never will. You just can't make me feel guilty enough to do something that I don't want to do. I don't get that feeling that supposedly gnaws at your conscience. Maybe I'm lucky? My mother never made me feel guilty of anything and I didn't grow up Catholic.

I also don't understand prayer. But, that's a topic for another writers' group.

I certainly don't understand why anyone in their right mind would choose to be a Republican. That's also a topic for another writers' group. (Hmmm, maybe I should join another writer's group?)

I also don't understand how we humans successfully communicate. Each of us grows up with a different way of how to look at things. Then as we meet in a classroom, in a store, on the street, we express our point of view and expect the other person to know just where we are coming from.

I don't understand why most bagels suck, why anyone would want to own an art gallery, why prisoners make license plates, and why most pizza sucks (not enough sauce, lousy crust,

crappy cheese, oh, I could go on).

I don't understand how electricity works or how hot water is just standing by at the twist of a faucet. Don't get me started on how toilets work. Because they don't always work and plunging them is just too disgusting.

I don't understand why supermarkets sell so many different brands of milk, granola or canned juice, and I surely don't understand why there's nothing better than an ice cold beer on a hot summer's day.

I do know why condoms suck. Because, "oh what a feeling" is lost between here and there.

I don't understand why someone invented the "bra." If only Hugh Heffner were still alive, maybe he could shed some light on the subject?

I don't understand why we pay for television programs, or, for that matter, why we tip a waiter.

I don't understand why we complain, why friendships sometimes end yet families stick together.

I don't understand highway signs in Florida, why most people don't pay any attention to the speed limit, why zippers get stuck, why a heated pool is always cold when you first get into it, why mosquito bites itch like crazy, why it's so easy to get fat and so hard to get skinny, why most TV commercials are so full of lies, why sex doesn't last longer, why a doctor's instructions sound like a Looney Tunes cartoon...

I don't understand why socks always get holes, why we think that life exists elsewhere and why some people just don't have a sense of humor.

But most of all, I don't understand what it means to die.

I Had a Dream

I had a dream. Not at all like the one Martin Luther King, jr. had. Actually, I've had lots of dreams. Haven't we all? Missing a class. Forgetting where the class is located. Falling .. oh, falling...showing up to work or school naked...your teeth are falling out...fear of failing a test... being chased... the mind plays so many scenarios when it's left to its own ramblings. How do you come up with these crazy ideas? Who writes these scenarios? Are we all really motion picture directors? How come we seldom remember them?

The dreams I seem to remember were recurring. As I look back, they all made quite a bit of sense. The most haunting dream went something like this: I lived with my family in a very large Victorian house. I might even describe it as huge. For some odd reason, it was divided into two completely different homes. The left side was just a normal house: living room, dining room, hallway, bedrooms, kitchen, bathroom..the standard stuff. The furniture was simple and comfortable. The ceilings and lighting were bright. We pretty much lived the life of Dick and Jane. Everyone was loving, food was plentiful and life was good.

Then there was the other side of the house. Nobody ever went over to the other side. It was dark. The front door was jammed. The rooms were furnished with couches and armchairs and rugs from the 1930s. I walked into that room once in a rare while. Looked around and left. Oh, I forgot to tell you the most bizarre thing about this "other side" of the house–The roof was totally decayed. The rafters were rotting. The black tar ceiling tiles were shredded and precariously hanging ready to fall at the next drop of rain. While I was never there during a rainstorm, it was clear it poured right through into the house.

I owned the house. I lived there for many years. I continued to visit that side of the house. But I never talked about it with my family. And I never attempted to fix the roof or call a roofer. I always woke up in a cold sweat.

It took me a good while to figure out what this nightmare was all about–until I stepped back and looked at my career. I owned my own business. We produced TV spots and corporate marketing films. It was what one would call a "project shop." You hunted for work. And, after many attempts, you landed a job. You produced it and handed over the final product to the client. The very next thing that crossed my mind was, "oh, I guess I'm out of business."

So I went back on the hunt for the next job. Sometimes it came fast. Sometimes I waited months for the next project. Fear set in as time passed. How would I pay my bills? It was a career path I chose. When the good times were good, they were great. And when the bad times were bad...the ceiling was falling.

Then I retired. And so did the dream...

I also had another recurring dream that haunted me for many years. When I was 19, I was drafted into the US Army. When my draft notice arrived my Dad said something I never heard him say before, "Oh, fuck."

My mother immediately called her brothers and sister in Montreal to see if I could move in with one of them. Since I didn't really have a plan for my life, I figured, "how bad could this be?"

I was young and didn't have a clue what to make of this situation.

The first four months were miserable. The worst days of my life. Being bossed around. Being told to do things I didn't want to do. Being told what kind of job I would have for the next few years. Being told where to live. It all totally sucked. But I hunkered down and 23 months and ten days passed pretty quickly(I was released slightly early to start college for the Fall Semester). On the last day I collected my DD214 (Honorable Discharge). It was my ticket to freedom.

About ten years later I had a dream. A letter in the mail. It was another draft notice. I opened it. I was to report to Ft. Hamilton in

Brooklyn in two weeks. I screamed, *"YOU'VE GOT TO BE FUCKING KIIDDING ME! I gave my two years. LEAVE ME ALONE!"* I woke up in a cold sweat. I'm not sure why this dream ended but I'm sure glad it did.

"Are you sure this isn't a nightmare? And that we won't just wake up?"

"Yes."

"Because dreamers always wake up and leave their monsters behind."

ALEXANDRA BRACKEN, *IN THE AFTERLIGHT*

I Never Thought I'd Live to See the End of the World

"You don't stop laughing because you grow older. You grow older because you stop laughing."

I'm 72 years old (almost 73). In teenage years, that means I'm just between being less ticklish and snoring much more often. I can walk a dog, take a nap, and skip a rock on a pond (although not necessarily in that order nor all at the same time). I can write and paint (not houses, mind you) but don't ask me to sing (unless you want my wife to burst out into laughter).

I've seen fire and I've seen rain (thanks, James Taylor) but I never thought I'd see my world come to a near complete stop–especially by a genome that is just 27 kilobases wide (yeah, go look that one up).

This lethal little thing has brought us to our proverbial knees. To date, we can't go to concerts, theater, movies, beaches, restaurants, parks or anything else that's fun to do. So we stay cooped up in our little hovels. The morning routines are pretty much the same...brush your teeth, take a shower, eat breakfast, and then come the questions born of tight quarters: Is that your pencil on the table? Does it really need to be there? Do you mind if I move that piece of paper to the other side of the house? Did you really leave your belly button lint on your napkin? Do you need the spaghetti sauce you put into the refrigerator yesterday?

And, then the fun begins, "so, what do you want to do today?"

"I dunno"

"Want to learn pinochle?"
"Wanna take the dog for a walk?"
"Wanna help me turn the mattress?"
"Isn't it time to clean under the house?"
"Or, get the cobwebs out of the chandelier?"
"Wanna watch the news?"
Oh, God .. just shoot me!
"Governor Cuomo, how long do you think the Coronavirus will be with us?"
"Months... months... MONTHS."

Well, that sure calls for a plan. But you know what Mike Tyson said about a plan? "Everyone has a plan until they get punched in the mouth." Hmmm.. maybe a plan is not what's in the cards. Maybe, just maybe, we need to be more zen...more existential about our day-to-day existence? Maybe we all need to become pinball machines. Pull the lever and keep bouncing around while fighting to stay alive for just a few more precious moments. But, wait...there's another ball, and another ball. Maybe Joni Mitchell was right? "The seasons, they go 'round and 'round, and the painted ponies go up and down, we're captive on the carousel of time."

Where we go from here is just a question of time. Will we return to the same place? Or will we take the fork in the road to wherever it might lead us?

> "Nothing puzzles me more than the time and space; and yet nothing troubles me less."

CHARLES LAMB

Hiding in Plain Sight

Here I am in Paradise Prison. It's really quite lovely. Two bedrooms, two baths. Plenty of toilet paper and wipes. A big kitchen with a big, well-stocked, refrigerator. A big screen TV and an art studio. Plus, a lovely view of a pond. We have very nice neighbors and the neighborhood is lovely. The grass and foliage are well groomed. The pest-control guy comes around on a regular basis. We just had all of the roofs cleaned by a company called "Fiddler on the Roof" (I'm guessing that somebody on our Board of Directors felt that their name had a certain je ne sais quoi). We have a small clubhouse where people play Mahjong, Poker, Billiards and Ping Pong. We also have an auditorium where we occasionally invite an entertainer to sing, dance or tell jokes. We have a lovely pool.

Then came an unwanted visitor to our corner of paradise. Not a burglar or a Peeping Tom or a car thief or anything like that. It was kind of a sci-fi visitor from who knows where? You couldn't see it, feel it, taste it, or touch it. But it was a menace for sure. It carries a nasty upper respiratory infection, and if it grabs you by the throat, there's a good chance you'll have seen your last sunrise. It's called Novel Coronavirus Disease (COVID-19).

So we went from paradise to prison. First our parks and golf courses were closed. Then our wildlife refuges. Then the authorities closed our non-essential businesses. Our restaurants were closed (sans take out). And then they told us to "stay in place" for six weeks. Then they closed our pool.

So we sit in our lovely paradise prison. We watch TV with news that gets bleaker and bleaker. And, we eat–breakfast, snack, lunch, snack, dinner, snack. We take our puppy out for a walk (but we must keep our distance from other dog walkers). We can't even sit on the bench by our pond (unless we're alone with our dog). Forget about having dinner with friends–unless we're eight feet apart. So, I spend my days writing wisecracks on Facebook. I'm convincing myself that I'm sharpening my comedic writing skills. Except it's harder and harder to be funny.

Maybe I'll have a different outlook in six weeks and miraculously turn a corner bursting into uncontrollable laughter? Or maybe I'll write about the end of the world?

Perfect World

    I want to live in a world where you always win your Solitaire game, where milk never goes bad, where you never have to double-knot your shoelaces, where you can always say exactly what you're thinking, where your washing machine always finds your dirty clothes and your dryer always folds them, where you can eat anything you want without guilt or consequences, where your TV reads your mind and opens up the right program at the right moment, where you never need new tires for your car, where a robot walks your dog and picks up the poop, where it's okay to have red spaghetti sauce at every meal, where procrastination is a way of life, where you can push a button and eject the guy in front of you in a movie theater or airplane, where the toilet seat knows if you need it up or down, where every meal is delicious, where everyone sniffs everyone else when they first meet, where your shower is the perfect temperature, where you only need to walk downstairs, where sex always feels like the first time, where your parents are always available for a nice warm hug, where you can visit the dead and then come back to the living…if only

    I want to live in a world where the coffee is always perfect, where ironing is unnecessary, where someone else always cuts the grass, where teachers know how to naturally communicate, where the sky is always blue and the clouds are always puffy, where you don't need a key to gain access, where pretty flowers are always blooming, where your bed is always made up after you wake up, where you always have hot water, where you never have to maintain any mechanical equipment, where you don't need to wear glasses for any reason, where you never get fat no matter what you eat, where our body exercises itself, where plugs of any sort don't exist, where your car converts into an airplane, where your oven/toaster oven/microwave oven and crock pot could all be built into one unit, where everyone knows the difference between good art and bad art, where everyone's uncle is funny, where there's only one type of men's underwear and one size fits all. If only...

I want to live where right and wrong are clear, where liars are banned to the Island of Elba, where hate doesn't exist, where everyone lives a free life and I'm the only one who consistently wins at the poker table..

If only...

Here's What I Don't Want To Be

When you get to be my age, you have plenty of time to think about what you might have wanted to be in your life: a doctor, a lawyer, an engineer, an architect...of course, the list could go on and on.

Or, if you're like me you might have wanted to be a circus acrobat (or a guy who just stood on top of an elephant in a three ring circus), a helicopter pilot, a boardwalk barker (oh wait, I did that back in high school) or a stand-up comedian.

I knew for sure I didn't want to be anything that required being serious all the time. So I ruled out being an actuary, a tombstone or insurance salesman, a zookeeper, or a barber.

My brother-in-law once sent me to a barber who seemed to be more interested in humping my shoulder than cutting my hair. But, that's a whole other story for another day.

I once thought it would be fun to be a bird. You could fly just about anywhere and poop on just about any car or bald head. What a way to spend your day...pooping and laughing. Or you could just hang out on a wire and talk shit all day with your friends.

I never really considered the salary of any job. That would have required too much adult thinking.

As it turned out, I went this way and that way. From a bunch of dumb jobs in high school, to another dumb job in the Army, to owning a psychedelic lighting store, to parking cars for rich and famous people at a restaurant in L.A. I drove a cab in NYC and worked at radio station downloading the local weather reports. And then to producing street festivals and another boring job at a university. And finally, making TV commercials. Boy was that fun!

Of course, for all of the things I wanted to be, I've thought long and hard about what I didn't want to be.

I don't want to be a blade of grass. And the reasons are pretty obvious: You get cut, stepped on, peed on, pooped on. You get all kinds of liquids poured onto you. You're always in a crowd, and, you're always subjected to the weather...rain, wind, snow, ice, tornadoes...

And worst of all...you can't do anything about all of these insults to your day-to-day existence.

So thinking back on it, maybe a circus acrobat wouldn't have been a bad choice?

I Shoulda Coulda Woulda

In 1962, I was 15 years old and I got invited to a party where there were girls. What did I know about girls? They didn't play poker. They didn't cut grass or shovel snow. They didn't play stick ball or stoop ball. Actually, I didn't know anything about girls. And here I was at a party with girls. Well, it didn't take long before they rounded up the boys to play Spin the Bottle. We sat down in a circle and set a bottle in the middle of the circle. It didn't take long for me to realize that this was some sort of kissing game.

All of a sudden I'm looking across the circle and there was the girl who I dreamed about in school. She was a cheerleader. The game started and before I knew it, it was my time to spin the bottle. Now, mind you, I never played this game before, but boy did my testosterone kick in when I saw that girl. I never gave much thought to the kind of bottle we were spinning. But, I soon realized we weren't spinning a round glass bottle. It was, in fact, a square glass milk bottle. Anyway, I grabbed the bottle in my hand and proceeded to spin it with all of my might. The bottle turned and twisted, danced on its side, flipped up in the air and crash landed into a mess of broken glass. I guess I wasn't too subtle about my early interest in this game. Too bad about my rock hard grip.

The party was not over though. We proceeded to another game called "Post Office." It wasn't really much of a game. The girls were in charge. They picked a guy and asked him what kind of "delivery" they wanted, pretty much anything from a Penny Postcard to a Special Delivery. Being a shy sort of guy I picked, you guessed it … a Penny Postcard.

Well, that was equivalent to a kiss on the cheek. The girl who picked me, who was clearly well equipped for more sophisticated services, told me I missed out, "You should have requested a Special Delivery."

To this day, I still wonder what she had in mind.

I shoulda coulda woulda...

Some years later I was in a movie theater with a first date. *It's a Mad, Mad, Mad, Mad World* was playing on the screen. About twenty minutes into the film I finally got the nerve to put my arm around her shoulder. My heart was pumping hard with all the jets wide open. Then, about fifteen minutes later my hand fell asleep. Even worse, it limped its way down over her shoulder and right onto her right breast. My hand was numb. I didn't feel a thing. But that excuse just didn't cut it. My mad, mad, mad, mad world turned into chopped liver for the night. Fortunately, there was a second, third, and fourth date. Thank goodness my hand stayed awake for all of the subsequent dates.

I shoulda coulda woulda...

It was News Year's Eve, 1968. I was living in Los Angeles. My friend Larry flew back home for a funeral. I had nothing to do, so I walked a few blocks over to the Playboy Club and asked them if they needed any help that night. They offered me a job as a Bartender's Helper. Well there I was in the fantasy place of all fantasy places for any red-blooded American boy. I was washing dishes. It was getting close to midnight. One of the waitresses asked me if I wanted to go to the After Hours party. Oh, was I excited! And, oh, was I tired! I went home after work to change my clothes, and fell asleep.

I shoulda coulda woulda...

I studied filmmaking at City University on Staten Island. In 1973, I applied to continue into Graduate School. I chose three universities; Temple University, NYU, and USC in Los Angeles. Since I was a mediocre student at best, I thought all of my choices would be considered a stretch. But since I produced a pretty good student film while I was studying at City University, my credentials carried some weight. Two out of the three universities accepted me. NYU said I could skip the first year of a three-year program. USC wanted to know why I wanted to study there since I already knew how to produce a film. During this time I got married and we had a baby. So I passed up on the film schools and got a graduate degree in performing arts management. No regrets. It all turned out well. I owned a film production company for 31 years.

I coulda ... I shoulda .. I woulda .. I did a ... good thing.

I Want To

I Want To ..

I want to wake up in the morning with a smile on my face.

I want to laugh...like the very first time it made my ribs hurt.

I want to touch the clothes that Martians wear.

I've always wanted to squeeze the Charmin.

I want to touch you where I can't.

I want to touch everything that reads "Do Not Touch."

I want to touch a Cubist Nude at the Metropolitan Museum of Art.

I want to live inside a Van Gogh painting.

I want to lick a Jeff Koons sculpture.

I want to touch the Statue of Liberty under her clothing and a nude Mona Lisa...just to compare and contrast.

I want to be a cute little dog who scares the crap out of a big fluffy cat.

I'd like to pee outside of the shower. Just because...

I'd like to be a stalk of asparagus for 3 days. Hey, it's a fast life.

And, just once, I think I'd like to walk to Hawaii.

Most of all, I want to do silly things everyday.

Preferably on Tuesdays...when no one is looking.

That's the day I'd like to spend with you-know-who. I'd like to have a good, long ticklefest with him. And then when we're done I'd like to do it again and again. Until it hurts.

And then, I'd like to punch you know who in the nose.

I'd like to have a pillow fight. Want to join me?

I'd like to taste something delicious...like ice cold Welch's Grape Juice on a hot summer's day.

I'd really like to fly like a hummingbird. Because she's the Queen on the chessboard. She can fly as far as she wants in any direction. Oh, would that be wonderful or totally confusing?

I'd like to dance. The Watusi would be fine but, I'd settle for a really sexy tango.

I'd like to spend the night with Bo Derick, Raquel Welch, and Sofia Vegara. Just to compare and contrast.

I'd like to land on Mars and start a new world. Hey, it's a big universe...somebody's got to start fucking it up.

I've Had Enough Virus Talk

Clearly our world has changed. There's a virus out there and it's causing harm. No doubt about it. You turn on the TV news, look at the newspaper, go on social media chat groups–it's talked about every day and everywhere. "Did you get your shot?"

"Do you know anybody who has a list of places to get it?"

"Did you get an appointment?"

"How far did you go to get it?"

"How long did you wait in line?"

And then the conversation sometimes goes: "Well, I heard ... you can die from the shot."

"And, I heard it's not very effective."

"My arm swelled up like there was a Gila Monster in there.."

"My aunt got the shot and it said it hurts like hell."

"There's a cop in Okeechobee who got the shot and now, he's got the virus."

"I'm not getting the shot. Everyone I know is not getting the shot."

ENOUGH. I'VE HAD ENOUGH.

And, then there's the TV news reports: "The UK is closed down."

"Poland is closed down."

"Disneyland is closed down."

Oh my God. The world is ending. "Few have the virus in New Zealand" (probably because few people come and go there).

All of a sudden we have a new word in our vernacular: mitigate. "There had been a provocation that mitigated the offense to a degree."

"If you want to be able to respond to things in a clear way, you must have a clear understanding of what we're talking about."

The baseline is endemic, epidemic and pandemic. WTF?

I don't know about you, but I'm ready for some new conversations. There have to be some subjects that need further exploration.

Have you ever had a high colonic irrigation? Is this something that American Indian women do in a corn field? Is it a religious cleansing ritual? Is there another way of describing this event?

"Mister, we're going to put a firehose in there to see what's what."

Okay, enough of that topic.

My mother once had a sebaceous cyst. I was probably 10-years old when she mentioned it. Those two words just went straight to my funny bone. The Coen Brothers found it funny enough to mention it in *Little White Lies* (Arthur is camped out in his living room draining his sebaceous cyst.). Maybe this was an ailment that only affected Jewish people?

Laugh??

I thought my pants would never dry.

My mother had a canasta friend named Nelda Zalenko. Some kids out there need to name their new rock band with her name. "Ladies and Gentlemen...'The Nelda Zalenko Light Orchestra'".

I'm sure I got this idea from Jeff Goldblum. He was once invited to bring his jazz trio to perform at the Café Carlyle in NYC. They asked him what the trio was called. Since they didn't have a name, he just came up with one. Named after his mother's friend, "The Mildred Schnitzer Orchestra." Too funny.

While I can't recall Nelda, I'm sure she bleached her hair bright red to match her bright red lipstick. The look perfectly fit her 1920s name.

My friend Neil had this almost-believable theory of the life of an inanimate object. It was a concept worth hearing out. Everything that sits still has some form of life inside of it. A rock, a table, a wall...everything. Neil owned a VW Bug. The radio didn't work. Well, it didn't work until you understood that it needed a wooden matchstick to jam into the corner of the apparatus. And voilà, 1010 WINS was yacking away. He also had a table lamp that suffered the same dilemma. Again, a matchstick jammed just below the light switch did the job.

So you see: there are lots more subjects to talk about than the virus. The good stories will last a long time. Hopefully, the virus will just go away.

Anything Can Be

"Listen to the mustn'ts, child.
Listen to the don'ts.
Listen to the shouldn'ts,
The impossibles, the won't.
Listen to the never haves,
Then listen to me....
Anything can happen child.
Anything can be."

SHEL SILVERSTEIN

For the first 20 years of my life I didn't think I could. Because I listened to the couldn'ts. You can't jump off that chair. You'll break your neck. You can't leave the refrigerator door open. You'll spoil the food. You can't skip that math test. You can't go to school without wearing underwear. You can't pick your nose because...well because. And, even if you could, you shouldn't. And, there was always a reason why you couldn't. Or so it seemed.

I grew up in a normal house where we followed the rules. We did everything by the book. No challenges. No variations. No hits. No runs. No errors. I remember being invited to my friend Robert's apartment for dinner. I didn't like what his mother made for dinner.

So I refused to eat it. "You can't refuse to eat my food." I didn't say a word to challenge her.

But I didn't eat her food. I was never invited back. Well, I guess yhat was my first challenge to "you shouldn't."

Now that I think about it, I did scream to all bloody hell when I was caged into a "playpen" when I was about 2 years old. So, I guess I just had that rebellious thing in me from the start.

When I was 7 or 8, my mother decided I needed piano lessons. All seemed to be going well until the teacher kept swatting the back of my hand with a ruler every time I hit a wrong note. Clearly, we had a different interpretation of what the right note was. Those lessons ended quickly. Come to think about it, I should have swatted her.

A few years later I took up the trombone. Again, all seemed to be going along pretty well. Until the music teacher told me you couldn't...you mustn't...you shouldn't. I must have had a deaf ear.

I didn't have a clue what he was talking about. Well, the Memorial Day Parade came and went. And so did my trombone career.

They say that the "age of reason" starts around age 7 or 8. I must have been a late starter, because I didn't challenge "reasoning" until I was 18 or 19. Of course, the timing wasn't exactly great. That's exactly when I got drafted into the Army and soon realized that this mustn't, shouldn't and couldn't went out the window. Because there were three ways to do things in the Army: the right way, the wrong way and the Army way. I had to defer my rebellious ways for a couple of years.

By then, the Age of Aquarius had begun. You could grow your hair. You could wear torn jeans. You could walk around in sandals. You could do whatever you wanted when you wanted. Well, as long as you could figure out how to earn some cash. It was a liberating time for me. If I found a good reason, I could do what I wanted to do and where I wanted to do it. There wasn't any mustn't, should't or couldn't. If you drove on the right side of the road and didn't speed, you were good to go on your merry way.

I followed my star and had a bunch of fun. I released the shackles of impossibilities and realized that anything was possible if you set your mind to it.

Now I'm in my later years. The mustn't, shouldn't, and couldn'ts take on a new definition. You shouldn't step over that parking bumper because you could trip. You mustn't forget to take your pills. You shouldn't go out without a walking cane. You mustn't eat that or you'll get constipated. You couldn't do 100 pull ups. Not in a million years.

In any case, I'm glad I found my mantra.

Anything can happen, child. Anything can be.

All of My Family Are Weirdos and All of My Friends are Quirky

When you get to be of a certain age a few things happen to you. Well, more than a few things, but I'll just focus on the ones that don't have anything to do with your plumbing.

You come to realize that your family is weird. And, that's precisely why you are weird. My Uncle Jack used to flush the toilet the first moment he arrived at our house from his long drive from Montreal. If he was satisfied with the flush all was well. His wife, my dear departed Aunt Esther, had a strange habit of chewing on her tongue. Yeah, it was like watching a cow chewing her cud. A very strange behavior.

My Uncle Morris never talked…he just performed. On Passover. He read the service from cover to cover on the holiday. It was an easy three-hour ordeal. I did my best to try and make him laugh. And, sometimes I succeeded. His wife, Aunt Anna, had this amazing cackle. It could pierce through the walls of their Bronx apartment…down the hall and up the stairs.

My Uncle Howard was this ample-bellied guy who wore very slick three-button vested suits. And he always carried a wad of cash. All rolled up with a wrap-around rubber band. He was always the generous fellow who picked up the check at a top-notch Jewish deli.

My mother was a piece of work. The baby of eight. Always a Dr. Jekyll and Mr. Hyde. Funny as all hell. Always ready with a great joke. Always burst out laughing just before she hit the punch line (it make her jokes even funnier). But, on her dark side, she always ragged on my father. She was never satisfied to let him be. And my Dad turned a deaf ear.

"He can't hear anything that I just said."

"No, that's not true. He just developed selective hearing."

My wife, oh, my wife. She's the least weird of the bunch. Well, she does spend an inordinate amount of time in the bathroom doing who-knows-what. And due to her worrying and nagging, she has a new family moniker. Her older brothers now call her Mom. On top of that I call her "Pollyanna." She always looks at the bright side of life. I guess there are benefits to not growing up Jewish.

And then there are my cousins. But they're still alive so I'll stay clear of those subjects to avoid any time in a courtroom.

My friends are just as weird. When you're in conversation with one of them it's like talking to a clam. One word answers. Few questions. And another gets into high gear conversation. She has many accomplishments. Her list is impressive and, at times, exhausting. Another one is a worry wart. She calls in the hospital report like a professional golf announcer, "first the doctor did this, then he did that. It was close, but he pulled it off." There's always a better doctor and a better hospital to do the job.

I have another cousin who I haven't seen in fifty years.

"Oh it would be so great to see you. But I can't see you in New York. Can we meet up in Florida?"

"Sure."

And, when she's in Florida, "I can't see you now. I'm going back to New York."

"I'll be in Nairobi in the Fall. Want to meet up on my safari?"

I have a former client who turned into a long time friend. We were working on producing a TV spot in Mendocino, California. It was about to turn sunset. He turned to me in the car and said, "Silverman, isn't this the most beautiful place you've ever seen?"

And, I responded with a deadpan face, "No, it sucks."

He looked at me. I looked at him. We both burst out laughing. That moment turned into a lifetime friendship.

I have an old friend who lives overseas. We have a history of texting nonsense. Anyone who reads our exchanges would wonder, really wonder..if it's early onset dementia or if we never graduated from elementary school. It's kind of our Pig Latin for old friends. We laugh and laugh and laugh.

Let's face it. Everyone is weird. Except for me. Okay, I do have a few strange habits.

Every Shirt Has a Stain and Story To Go With It

I'm a little overweight. Okay, maybe not just a little. Because I like to eat, I'm mostly okay with that. Except...I suffer from "chest of drawers syndrome." Everything I eat goes from my chest to my drawers. Coffee, pasta sauce, balsamic vinegar, beef stew, pizza–you name it. Every food has an equal opportunity to travel south on my shirt.

I guess you could say I'm a *schlemiel*. You know the difference between a *schlemiel* and a *schlimazel*? A *schlemiel* spills stuff on himself. A *schlimazel* spills it on someone else.

So, what is a *schlemiel* to do? Grab a dish towel, or a placemat, or a tablecloth (well that's a little big), and cover yourself when you're eating. Well that's all well and good, but what do you do with all of the spills that land on those coverings? It's the same dilemma.

Alas, there is a solution, albeit not one that's "on the spot," if you'll excuse the pun. My dear, sweet wife takes stain removal to a high art. She could be a Stain Remover Tester for Tide, Resolve, OxiClean– you name it. She's tested the sprays, the rub-ons, and the stain-removal sticks. When she conquers a particular stain, she celebrates like she scored a field goal.

It's truly a sight to behold.

Lately, I think I've come up with the perfect solution for a fella like me. Design a series of dinner shirts with different stains printed on the belly area–in full-blown color. Keep your sport jacket closed until you eat. And then open the button. Once you share the laugh with your dinner guests you can eat and drink to your heart's delight. Scrambled eggs with hot sauce, roast pork egg foo young with that delicious brown sauce, pasta with vodka sauce .. go man , go.

My Refrigerator

I don't want to live in my refrigerator. Not now. Not ever. If for no other reason–it's too cold in there. I moved to Florida to get away from the cold. I'm pretty happy at 75 degrees, but I don't think that Mary Anne's big tub of Greek yogurt would agree with me. Unless she changes her requirements and can live with a few curdles.

The other big reason why I don't want to live in my refrigerator is that it would be difficult to figure out where I would fit in. You all know I'm kind of an oddball. Yet, my refrigerator seems to be a place for conformists. Or at least "birds of a feather," if you know what I mean. The fruits live in one compartment The cheese in another. The veggies in another. The juices live on the balconies. The question is, did I ever ask them if they would get along during their short lives?

I can't imagine the Swiss cheese liking the Roquefort. Man, he stinks. I'm not even sure, if he took a shower in the sink, if Roquefort would pass the muster smell test. At best, it's kind of an arranged marriage, "we'll live together until the munster, cheddar and brie children grow up and move out of here."

It's kind of the same in the veggie compartment All's fine and good with the cukes, radishes, celery and tomatoes…until the arugula moved in. Who ever invited that legume? "We just can't live near this guy. I don't know if he's Indian or Latin but, this sexy, spicy fellow just doesn't belong here. He keeps rubbing against us, and causes all kinds of flutter.

The condiments are an altogether other thing. There are the preserves, the jellies, the mustards and ketchups. And, the weirdos like the jalapeño pepper spread, chili bacon jam, and pink lemonade jam. These guys are the headbangers of the fridge. They all have some kind of hairy stuff hanging from their caps. Maybe it's because they only get called on every once in a while.

The milk and juices? Forget about it. Did you ever try to mix these two? Feh. They're like oil and water. It's a good thing they live in sold cardboard containers. Otherwise, it would be a Splash War.

The butter lives on its own balcony in its own glass container. She's a lucky girl. Other than adjusting to everyone else's smell, she manages to live a private life. Well, that is until some human breaks in and stabs her. Too bad nobody gets out alive.

Maybe my refrigerator is a metaphor for life? Nah ... it's too cold.

Fascination

"Top to bottom, side to side, corner to corner. All you have to do is roll a ball...under the glass and over the bump...it falls in a hole...It lights a light...and then you roll a ball again...You don't have to go to college to read the book of knowledge to know... Now is the time, this is the place, the name of the game is 'Fascination.' It's just like 'Screeno,' 'Lot-o-Lucky,' or any of the five-in-a-row games. Five lights in any straight line or row, and you too could be the very next winner!"

The Boardwalk circa 1962 in Long Beach, NY was the place to go during hot summer nights. You could go for a nice walk and catch an ocean breeze. If it was July 4th, you'd see a pretty good fireworks show that was projected from a barge out in the ocean.

I was a Boardwalk Barker at a game called 'Fascination,' a competitive electronic bingo game.

44 tables, 10 cents to play. I sat on a high seat overlooking the players. Once we had 44 players seated, I flipped a switch and the game began. The first player to beat all others at getting 5 balls in row was the winner. And from the start of the game, I just blabbed and blabbed to hustle the game to the next 44 players who would be walking by on the Boardwalk.

"Hey, there's a player going for the top red line. It's up and around... oh, right next door! He just missed winning 8 big, *big*, coupons or 800 Plaid Stamps just for a dime's win! Right next door is Izzy's Delicious Knishes. One coupon buys you a knish .. cherry cheese, potato, kasha or pineapple just for a dime's win!"

It was amazing to me how people like to play games and compete with one another just to win a little stuffed animal or a knish. Then again, those knishes were always hot and delicious.

Great Minds

What is a great mind? Is it a deep thinking mind from many centuries ago? Or a mind you met just today? Is it great if it rattles off great puns? Is it a great mind hidden deep inside a bum on the bowery whose mind hit on hard times. Do all scholars have great minds even if they don't know how to tie their shoes? Maybe it's a mind that was sent to prison for standing its ground. It's not so easy to define a great mind.

I'm not sure I ever met a "great mind." I've met famous people and terrific teachers, doctors and lawyers and politicians (even some with great minds), artists who amazed me with their vision and skills. I've studied Socrates and Plato, but that was long ago, at a time when their words were way over my head. I guess they were great minds, but I didn't know that at the time.

I've met advertising writers who were clever, and journalists who were smart. I've met dogs with great instincts (or so it seemed). If you just pay attention, you can learn a lot from a dog. I've met children who have expressed great innocent wisdom, and janitors who know more about life than most of those who are well-educated.

I'm lucky to say I have a few friends with great minds. Yes, they were good students who followed the rules and they had very successful careers. But more so, when they retired, their great minds began to really flourish.

I know a teacher named Joe who became a photographer. He loves nature and the street life of New York City. His photos tell great stories of the poor who find hope and joy from just a moment in time. He captures their laughter, their achievements, and their everyday experiences that make life so sweet. His nature photos capture...nature, in all of her glory. He makes me look at life through his looking glass, and my day is always better after I see what he sees.

I had a janitor when I owned a small building in Richmond, Virginia. His name was Nathaniel. What a sweet man. He was quiet, reliable, and very thorough doing his work. On occasion, we would chat about race relations. In his spare time, he ministered to his flock in a small church. We talked about the days of old in Richmond when life was very hard, and we talked about the progress that's been made. While the scars still remain, his heart is filled with hope for a better tomorrow. I will always remember his optimism. And to me, that is a great thing to share with your churchgoers and the people who pass through your life.

I had a teacher named Joseph Caruso. He was a retired US Army Sergeant. I think he taught Seventh Grade. John deeply loved to teach American History. At one point, we were learning about South Carolina before the Civil War. To illustrate his point, he would stand up on top of a desk and bellow out the words of John C. Calhoon, an American statesman and political theorist from South Carolina who served as the seventh vice president of the United States. To me, he took a dry subject and brought it to life. I'll never forget his enthusiasm. It was a great sight to see.

Once I met an advertising copywriter in Nashville, Tennessee. I was showing a group of creative folk our film production demo reel. Afterwards, we stepped into his office and I innocently asked him, "What makes a great copywriter?"

He replied, "It's all about someone who understands human nature."

Just a few short words, but what a profound thought.

My dear wife surely has a great mind. After all, she chose me to be her husband. Apart from that moment of greatness, she's a voracious reader and is beaming with kindness and intelligence. To me, she was one of very few great and very caring nurses. To know how to heal a wounded soul is indeed someone with a great mind.

She has a wonderful, hearty laugh. Only someone with a great mind can enjoy a moment like she does.

My old and dear friends Mike and Fred both have great, clear-thinking minds. Both are funny. Both are well read. Both are great students of contemporary culture. And both are wonderful punsters. Their great minds keep my trying-to-be-great mind alive and curious.

And then I met a guy named Stan, a meteorologist, student of classical piano, and another fabulous punster. His greatness lies in his warmth, his sense of humor and his astounding knowledge of the universe. I really love spending time with him. And I hope some of his greatness rubs off on me one day.

Well, I don't know if I truly addressed the assignment, but, I had fun writing this little ditty.

Cliché Love

I was sitting in the student lounge talking to a friend about nothing. Or maybe I was staring at the wall. Or something like that. And out of the blue comes this tall, attractive, brunette.

"Something in the way she moves attracts me like no other lover."

She had me at hello. We talked for a while. I can't really say I remember the conversation. But you know what they say? Everything happens for a reason.

I don't really know what we talked about. Back in those days, my brain and sex drive were just intertwined. Somewhere in her smile she knows that I don't need no other lover. After a while, I asked her if she wanted to come to my class. She politely declined. Well, that was that...that was all...that was it? Was it finished?

So I thought, until I found her outside my classroom. So, I said to myself, "this looks like something big is going to happen."

"Could it be?
Who knows?
There's something due any day
I will know, right away
Soon as it shows..."

But I was shy. Until she said, "Keep calm and kiss me." Well, uh...gee...that was pretty good.

> *"Oh yeah, I'll tell you something*
> *I think you'll understand*
> *When I'll say that something*
> *I want to hold your hand"*

The next thing you know, we had our first date. I invited her to my empty apartment. Both of my roommates had recently moved out. As it turned out, I didn't have to worry about finding the right words. We just jumped into action. As they said in *Ferris Bueller*, "Life moves pretty fast. If you don't stop and look around once in a while, you could miss it."

The only thing in the apartment was...my bed. I didn't exactly know what to say.

"The first thirty seconds of any conversation or presentation are like the last two minutes of a football game. This is when victory or defeat is determined, the period of time when your audience is deciding whether you are interesting enough for them to continue paying attention. Say just the right thing, and the communication game is yours. Your audience gets hooked, and they're enticed to hear what you will say next. Get it wrong, and your listeners start daydreaming, checking their smartphones, or plotting their conversational exit strategy."

Well, one thing led to another. We dated a few more times and then we moved in together.

> *"Me and you and you and me*
> *No matter how they toss the dice, it had to be*
> *The only one for me is you, and you for me*
> *So happy together."*

First it was with her two nursing student roommates in a one-bedroom apartment. Yeah, that lasted about a month. And then we moved into a hippy commune.

> *"To everything (turn, turn, turn)*
> *There is a season (turn, turn, turn)*
> *And a time to every purpose, under heaven"*
>
> **THE BYRDS**

And then to our own apartment in NYC.

> *"Some folks like to get away*
> *Take a holiday from the neighborhood*
> *Hop a flight to Miami Beach or to Hollywood*
> *But I'm takin' a Greyhound on the Hudson River line*
> *I'm in a New York state of mind."*
>
> **BILLY JOEL**

Then to Staten Island, where I went to finish my undergraduate degree in sociology and filmmaking.

We moved into another hippy commune. I drove a cab. I smoked some pot. I graduated and took a job producing street festivals and ferry concerts.

Then we got married. The Sicilians came. The Jews came. The old friends came. The hippies came. It was a lovefest of the first order.

> *"Love and marriage, love and marriage*
> *It's an institute you can't disparage*
> *Ask the local gentry*
> *And they will say it's elementary"*
>
> **JIMMY VAN HOUSEN**

Henry Hudson Park

I was sitting in the park the other day. It was just around dusk. My wife and I were chatting with a neighbor about this and that. There was a Little League Game going on just down the hill. The field was starting to get a little dark when all of a sudden the park lights turned on.

And then in a flash, they went off.

A minute later, they went on. And then they went off. This sequence continued for about eighteen minutes. First, it was weird. Then, it was strange. And then, I became convinced there was a Park Service employee who was having a little fun. On...off...on...off...on...off. Working in this park can definitely be a boring job. So why not have a little fun on a spring afternoon? The kids continued to play ball. We continued to chat about this and that. It all went along pretty smoothly until it became annoying. But, nobody seemed to ask, "hey, what's going on?"

So, I was wondering ... are we all so numb to practical jokes that they no longer have any meaning? Did anyone wonder what the hell was going on? Or, was it just a timer that went array? Maybe this happens every night? Maybe the night critters come out and have a party?

The skunks, possum, coyotes, rats, mice, and whoever else lives there. What about the homeless guy who owns a cell phone and a computer? Maybe he's the cause of this mischief? Nah. He hasn't been seen in the park so far this year.

Rumor has it, he owns a big house and has a ton of money. So I guess it's possible he lives to play practical jokes on people in the park. Hey, it could be. While most of us live our lives in quiet desperation, this guy seems to dance to a different drummer. Maybe he just buys and sells stocks? Maybe he's an online life coach? Maybe he's plotting a new world order? Who knows? If he shows up again, I just might grab a seat on his bench and see what makes him tick.

I like cruising around the park. You meet all kinds of people and their dogs. One guy lives in a Charlotte Bronte House with a commanding view of the Hudson River. He's smart, friendly, and has a cute little dog. Another guy meets up with him and has a very tall dog. You'd think the little one would be afraid of him. Nope. They wrestle. And, the little one often gets on top. The big one is big enough to swallow the little one in one bite. But it's just a sweet encounter. Two unlikely looking friends who like to play-fight.

Then there's Madeline and Mocha. Madeline is in her 90s and Mocha is probably about ten or twelve. Madeline is a Holocaust survivor. It seems like they've been together forever. They walk about a mile around the park everyday. And they take a seat on one of the benches. Madeline seems to know everyone, and Mocha seems to bark at everyone. He's pretty small and compact. Doesn't seem to bite. But he sure can make a lot of noise.

We passed three spry older women huffing it up the hill. A woman called out to one of them. "Hi Gloria."

She looked at me as she passed and said her name wasn't Gloria, but she'll accept it as an acknowledgment. I called her Sally. She said that's fine, too.

We used to walk by a lovely older Black man who sat on the bench. We always exchanged pleasantries. I'm guessing he was retired and just enjoyed a good, relaxing sit by himself.

Then there's the lovely mailman (well, mailwoman). She parks her rolling mail cart by her side and carves herself a spot on a bench just before lunch time. She's always chatting on her cellphone in Spanish, but always takes the time to say hello.

Miriam often enters the park with her big, old, and sick dog. Both have health issues. Both seem to help each other make it through the day.

Shelly also has a big older dog. Shelly also has health issues. If you ask her how she's doing, her response could easily occupy the rest of your day.

And then there's Dan, the new and very cute little puppy, and a Romanian woman who works from home has a sweet companion dog.

Some people stop for a chat. Some people don't stop at all. I wonder if Henry Hudson would walk a dog in his namesake park? Ahoy, Little Hudson. Time to do your business.

Crossing Paths

In the early '80s, I owned a Victorian-style house in Richmond, Virginia. It was a lovely 2-story building constructed in the early 1900s. I used the downstairs rooms for our film production offices and I rented the upstairs rooms. My office was in the front of the building facing the street.

The neighborhood was located in between downtown Richmond and the main campus of Virginia Commonwealth University. Most of the businesses in the area were somehow related to the advertising industry. Graphic artists, printers, photographers and ad agencies. My building was located on Cary Street, a feeder street for commuters to find their way to their office building parking lots. It was one-way and had few traffic lights. Since there were so few retail businesses within a 10-block range, you seldom saw any pedestrians walking by.

We didn't produce any TV spots or programs at or near our office. It was just a place to sit by a phone to set up some appointments and do some basic editing. Our office was quiet and rarely had any visitors.

One late morning in the spring of 1987, an African-American man quickly entered our building. He was, more or less, about 5'8" and 160 lbs. He wore average blue-collar clothing and had a short haircut. What distinguished him from most people who I occasionally crossed paths with were his demeanor, his style of breathing, and his eyes.

The moment he entered my building, I got up and met him in the hallway. He looked back-and-forth like a scared cat. The palms of his hands spread out as if he were a spider about to crawl up the wall. To say that I was a bit concerned would be an understatement. I started to breathe heavily, and he was breathing heavily, "Mister, I was just let out of jail. I need bus money to get back to New Jersey. I don't have any money, and I don't want to hurt you. What can I do to make some money?"

Many of us are very jaded when we cross paths with seemingly-desperate men. Sometimes we wonder why they don't just get a job as a dishwasher? Or a grass cutter? Or some other menial job that can carry them over from day-to-day? Of course, my wife often reminds me that you need an address to secure a job and these people live on the street.

Clearly, this guy was desperate. He seemed to have an immediate need and a short fuse. I said, "Wait here." I briskly walked to the back of my building and handed him a broom. "Sweep the steps and sidewalk outside my building and I'll pay you." He grabbed the broom, exited the building, and proceeded to sweep the dust and dirt away. When he finished, he re-entered my building, handed me the broom and stood still. I handed him some money. He looked down and thanked me. And that was the last time I ever saw him.

What kind of society are we to release a prisoner without any money, with a prison record and few employable job skills? Well, that was the case in Virginia back in the 1980s. Hopefully things have changed.

Technology

Does technology make your life easier? I don't know.

I tried to make an appointment with my doctor. In the old days, you called their office and scheduled an appointment. Easy peasy. These days you need to be a computer genius. Go onto the doctor's office website. Type in your username and password. WAIT. Who has a username and password for their doctor's office? Maybe I set one up four years ago. Username: drpokeme? Password: Ibreakyourface2ZK? No. That doesn't work. Here we go with the setup new username and password. And of course you need to fight with their website because you didn't type an Upper *AND* Lower Case Letter. And Z is not acceptable. Do it again. And it is rejected. Do it again. And, it is rejected again. *AGGGGH!!*

I think I'll try to schedule an airline flight. But, instead of going to the airline's website I'll go to Expedia or some such intermediary. This time they try to hook you into using their site by asking you questions about your travel plans. Even before you can determine if this is the best place to look for deals. Where are you going? When are you going? Who's going? How many travelers? Is it okay to sit next to a fat guy who farts? Do you mind sitting next to a window so you have to wake up the two people next to you so you can go pee? Do you mind if we give you a used wipe for your table? (We're trying to save money). Would you like a seat that doesn't crush your knees into your chin? Two more inches will cost you $200.

Have you tried to order groceries on-line? Go to the grocery store's website. Username and Password. *ARRRRGH.* Once you get to the website you get to see what's available for delivery. I want fresh cherries.

You can buy 1–100. How many would you like? Do you want today's cherries or yesterday's cherries? Artichokes? Big ones, medium or small ones? Sharp tips or cut? From California or Uzbekistan? Fresh fish? Still flapping or just laying there in ice? With the head or without? What we received today or last week? Does it matter if it smells?

Have you ever downloaded the Uber app? Click on it. No username or. password. *YAY!!* Where are you going? Do you mind if we load the car with 16 other riders? Are you in a rush? Take a look at our map. We'll pick you up at the corner next to the seedy bodega that's next to the Blood Donation Center. The driver's name is Nahamarando. He's driving a Blue Russian BMW.

Have you tried to book a parking spot in a NYC garage? Go on their site. No username or password. When do you want to park here? How long do you want to stay here? If you return one minute late we charge for an extra five hours. When you arrive at the garage it's not unusual for the garage attendant to tell you he doesn't have any spaces left. This is like the Seinfeld routine: "Did you get my reservation?"

"Yes. But, we don't have any spaces."

"Do you understand what a reservation is all about?"

"Yes."

"You are supposed to hold the space until I get there."

"Don't be a wise guy."

"I'm not being a wise guy."

"Well, the most important part of the reservation is that you hold the reservation. The taking of the reservation is the easy part."

I could go on and on about paying for a parking spot using the keypad in the parking lot. It's powered by a solar panel. You can just imagine how reliable that is. Or ordering a specialty pizza. You want chicken and pineapple on your pizza? Really? Or trying to order from a delivery intermediary like GrubHub. Which store are you ordering from? We don't work in that delivery area.

As you can tell. I'm not a big fan of using technology to make my life easier. Give me a rotary phone any day of the week.

The Commune

It was 1973. Mary Anne and I were living together in what we called a commune on Staten Island. It was actually a nine-bedroom Victorian house that seven college students all found at just about the same time. So we did what any kid who was looking for cheap lodging did in those days...we all agreed to move in together. It was an interesting group, to say the least. Two brothers were from Brooklyn. One was a little off center. The other was dead center. Personality-wise, that is. One often danced naked to Cat Stevens music. The other was quiet and hung around with his girlfriend.

One girl was from Queens who only ate macrobiotic food. It seemed to make sense when we realized that her father owned a fish store. Oh, the smells he must have brought home...another guy was also from Brooklyn. He liked marajuana... for breakfast, lunch and dinner. And a girl named Siobhan Lubieniecka. Cute as a button with a name that filled all four corners of her mouth. She was skinny as a rail and talked and talked and talked.

Another guy named Morgan hailed from Long Island. He looked like a member of the Hells Angels. Long hair, big black beard. His looks were deceiving though. He was a real mush.

Michael was also from Long Island. He was a quiet, sweet guy who looked like any kid who went to Woodstock.

And, then there was John. He danced to a different drummer. An early follower of Yoga, Buddhism, and all that seemed to bring you to the light. It was a lively group who got along amazingly well.

Once we settled in we realized we needed a phone. With seven or eight or nine different overnighters we realized the phone bill could get complicated. Someone needed to put their name down on the account. Yeah, right? Who had a credit history when you were in your 20s?

So the phone company came up with an idea. Could we be a company or an organization? If so, we could have a payphone installed. Bingo. John said, we'll tell them we're an Indian Tribe and name it after the street we live on: The Phelps Place Tribe. It was a perfect idea All you needed was a sock full of quarters every time you made a call. Well, that is until one of the "tribesmen" heard about a way to stick a pin through one of the phone wires so we could bypass the requirement for any coins. We didn't consider it unethical or illegal, but rather student ingenuity.

After living together for a while someone got the ridiculous idea that we should all invite our parents to visit us. Oh boy, that was an eye opening experience. Somewhat akin to having a party of strangers who were Trump and Bernie die hard supporters all in one place. They traveled from Brooklyn and Long Island...Catholics, Jews and Atheists. They left their comfortable middle class homes to see how a bunch of oddball kids could live together in a creaky old house on Staten Island–a borough that oddly seemed suitable. They explored the living room with a toilet that served as a seat. And a kitchen that had the strangest containers of leftover mung bean casserole and expired milk containers. Upstairs were the bedrooms. A mattress here, a mattress there...a large Indian scarf divides a room in two. Guitars here and there and everywhere. Let's just say it was a funny, crazy and weird place and a weird day.

Allow me to backtrack first. We were living together, and Mary Anne's parents weren't all too happy about that situation.

"What should we tell the family about you two? That you're shacking up?"

My reply to my father-in-law: "No, I wouldn't say that."

Him: "So what would you call it?"

Me: "Why don't you tell them we're living together?"

Him: "What the hell's the difference"?

Me: "It sounds better."

That wisecrack didn't fly so well.

Of course there was another illuminating conversation we had a few months later.

He: "So, are you going to marry my daughter?"

Me: "It's a possibility."

That one didn't fly so well, either.

Over time, and after we got married, the conversations drifted towards his oddball collection of electronics from the 1950s. I always thought he should write a book about how to cope with your Sicilian mother-in-law who lives in the room behind the kitchen.

After our Parent's Visiting Day, I decided to turn that event into a movie. It was a perfect project for a student studying the art of filmmaking. I hooked up with a friend to write the script, gathered up a crew from fellow students, acquired all of the camera/sound and lighting equipment that City University had to offer and off I went. First was casting talent from the local pool of community actors, next was a shooting schedule and off we went. A few days on location at our Victorian house, a few weeks in the editing room and voila. The premiere (and, only public showing) included the cast, crew, friends and the families who made the original event happen. *Uggh.* Who's idea was this? Maybe it wasn't such a great idea to show off the fiction version of the non-fiction event? I think there was some kind of applause at the end. On a positive note, the film helped me to get admitted to NYU and USC Graduate Film Schools. Too bad I never took either of them on their offers. The idea of making a living as a filmmaker was daunting in the early 1970s. So I got a graduate degree in performing arts management.

Bad Habits

I can't change my bad habits. There, I said it. I'm 75 years old and I've finally realized that my bad habits are what make me...me. And I don't really think my bad habits are so bad.

What's the big deal if I bite your nails? I'm sure dinosaurs did it. Or at least gorillas, orangutans, and monkeys do it. Well, if they don't they should. Who needs a stupid nail clipper? Mine is built-in. My teeth do the job just fine. Okay, so it looks kind of weird when I'm doing "the trim" in public. It often looks like I've just finished eating ribs and I'm savoring the leftover sauce. Except I always need to figure out what to do with the clippings. But, even if you use a nail clipper you have that same problem. Unless you're someone who spits them out. Now that's a bad habit on top of a bad habit.

Another one of my bad habits has to do with passwords. Everything I've read tells me that I shouldn't repeat any previous passwords. So, every time I'm asked for a password I create a new one. And then...they ask me to type it again. Do you think I remember what I just created? Would you remember "KissMyTuh66Duh?" Or "ShutuM66Duh?" I don't know about you, but I can't remember a password for more than one second. So, you'd think I would write it down? What a great idea—except I never remember which letters were capitalized. After you get it wrong on the 3rd pass, you're told that you can't get back into their site for 24 hours. 24 hours later I forgot my Username. I hate passwords.

Now here's a bad habit that doesn't seem so bad. I have a long standing agreement with my wife about dirty dishes. Whoever cooks, the other person washes the dishes. For the most part this deal works pretty well. Except I won't wash dishes until 10:00 PM. My logic? If I wash them sooner, it ruins the memory of a lovely meal. This deal doesn't always work between a person with OCD and a procrastinator. So when 9:00 PM rolls around, the OCD person sometimes jumps in to fight the decaying food plates. Once I raise my hand to contest, the dishes are already done. Maybe I could move up my rule to 9:45 PM? Or maybe not. After all, I still have a solid, lingering, memory of a wonderful meal.

I also have some bad bathroom habits. But I'll save those for when we alll smoke a lot of pot and get into a bathroom stupor.

I've always been a wise guy. It's just in my blood. I find most "senior" conversations extremely boring. They talk about too many aches and pains, too many hospitalizations, too many "one-up man" experiences; "well, you think you went through some shit, you need to hear my shit."

Or they talk about politics, or property taxes, or whatever. The only way I can turn the tide of these boring conversations is to throw in a left field comment: "Did you hear what Howard Stern said last night?"

That usually turns the tide. Or they ignore me and get right back to talking about what they were talking about. That's the point where I signal my wife it's time to head home. She usually gives me "the look," but agrees to leave within the hour.

Here's a bad habit that most of us share; I have a hard time changing my eating habits. I like what I like. Try something new? Maybe, but I'm sure I won't like it at a certain age. You just know which foods give you pleasure. I love Welch's Grape Juice. Every time I drink a small glass of the stuff I get a pleasure orgasm in my brain. It's like no other drink. Last week Mary Anne found a 2-for-1 special at Publix. That's a double orgasm. Wow! I also like green olives with stuffed pimentos.And cheese...just about any kind. But ask me to eat boiled okra. No way. Or calf's liver. Ugh. Well I'm still open to trying new foods, but I'm pretty sure I won't like them.

Listening: not my greatest strength. If someone doesn't engage me right away in a conversation or reading or lecture, I tend to drift off.

I think there's a connection between changing my food habits and changing my listening habits. I have to like it or understand what I'm hearing, or else I drift off into Never Never Land. That doesn't always sell well when my wife is talking to me. What do I drift off into? Sometimes, I look out the window to see if any women are wearing bikinis by the pool. That's always a great diversion. How I earned a graduate degree from New York University is still a mystery to me.

I have many more bad habits. Too many to rant about today. Maybe we're all bad habit-ers?

Maybe it's just human nature. Maybe we're just a bunch of selfish shits.

It's possible, you know.

My Good Friend Neil

Life has a mysterious way of matching people up. I was in Jones Beach on Long Island, sitting on the beach with friends. It was 1969. A guy comes along with his crowd and says, "Where should we sit?'

I looked up and said, "Sit here."

This guy's name was Jeff. He was a happy-go-lucky guy with a great sense of humor. We spent most of the afternoon laughing. One thing led to another and we realized we lived near each other in Queens. From there I met his friend, Neil...also a very funny guy. I dunno. Maybe it was the mood or the pot or whatever, but we soon became fast friends. Neil was a filmmaker. Just a hobby. He was making a film and asked me if I wanted to be in it. I said, "what do I have to do?"

He said, it's just a party scene. Look like you're having fun. Gee, that was tough. I said, "sure".

Neil finished editing the film and said to me, "how would you like to help me with the sound?"

I said, I don't know anything about sound for film. He said, "you work for a radio station. I'm sure you know more than I do about sound."

I liked that about Neil. He was direct, confident, and also happy-go-lucky.

But first, let's have some barbecued chicken. I said, "Neil, I'm not much of a chicken fan."

He said,"Oh, you'll like my chicken!"

I repeated: "I'm not much of a chicken fan."

He insisted. He cooked it. Blackened, before blackened was a cooking style. We ate it. He said, "So, how was it?"

I said it tasted like chicken. We both laughed.

Back to the film: Neil edited the film—it was a story about a girl who was caught in a bad cycle. She wanted friends. She wanted love. She turned to food. There wasn't any dialogue. Her fail attempts at reaching people coupled with her angst told the story. My job was to find music that enhanced the mood.

Neil handed me a print of the film and his 16mm film projector. I lived in an artist's loft above a movie theater a few blocks from the beach where I grew up. The loft was pretty large with a staircase that went up one flight to the corner of the room (the ceiling was probably 18 feet tall). I set up the projector next to my bed and projected the film all the way across the loft to the far wall. I had a turntable with an amplifier to play records while the film played. I had a stack of LPs. I tried one, another, a third, a fourth, a fifth record. Nothing seemed to fit the film. And, then I played "In-A-Gadda-Da-Vida" by Iron Butterfly. Oh, my. From the first frame of the film and the first note of the record it all fit like a glove. I think they call this kind of thing serendipity. We had a marriage.

This was the start of my film career.

Simca

It was a nice sunny day in Cleveland, Ohio. It was 1967 and I was in the Army, stationed at a nuclear missile base. This was my day off duty. I had recently bought a Simca...a car that cost me $400. That was a lot of money in those days when I was only earning $82 a month. It was a five-speed with all gears on the driver's column. Really fun to drive. When the salesman closed the deal he said, "Now, listen to me...don't tow anything behind this car."

Yeah, right? I was out for a drive with my friends. One of them needed a tow. We hooked up his car and off we went. We climbed a pretty big hill...haltingly chugging up the hill. We just about reached the peak when we heard an explosion. The engine must have burst at the seams. White smoke was billowing out of the hood. We all jumped out pretty quickly and simultaneously burst out laughing. It was a sight to behold. That was the end of my Simca days.

The Noise

"Did you hear that?"

"Hear what?"

"That sound."

"What sound?"

"Oh, come on. You're the one who can hear a cotton ball hit the ground from 2,000 feet up."

Dead air.

"There it is again."

"What?"

"That sound."

"What are you talking about?"

"Listen…every time you step on the gas there's a sound as if a high-pitched car horn is being tapped."

"You're crazy."

"Wait. There it is again. Just as you come to a stop."

The same beep beep.

"Do you hear it?"

"Sort of. But, what's the big deal?"

"The big deal is that this sound has been happening in our car for the past 10 months. And, it's just not normal for a car to make an inconsistent sound like that on a regular basis."

Clearly, something is wrong.

So, I looked up this problem on the internet:

"The Subaru Outback is known for it's cabin noise due to its open wagon design and lightweight construction. Some common noise complaints include:

- Road Noise: This noise can be amplified by the Outback's design and can distort The car's audio system.
- Tire Noise: This noise can be reduced with a wheel well sound deadening treatment.
- Rattling Noise: This can be caused by the ball joints, struts or strut mount, or a problem with the sway bar links.
- Grinding Noise: This is the sound of brake pads scraping against brake rotors, which can get damaged if these two parts keep rubbing together."

"There it is again. Beep beep. And, there it is again when you turn left."

"Beep beep. And, it even comes up when you turn right. I tell you it's making me crazy. I'm going to take the car into a local car repair shop and get to the bottom of this problem."

"Hi, can I help you?"

"Yeah, I've got this noise."

"What kind of noise?"

"Well, it sounds like a horn that's shorting or a metal thingy that rubs over another metal thingy.

But, it only happens sometimes. When I step on the gas and when I take sharp turns and when I come to a stop."

"Come back on Monday and I'll take a whack at it."

Well, by this time, curiosity was killing me. So my wife said let me take a look under the driver's seat.

"Are you crazy? This could be a serious problem. It could be the struts or the brake pads and you're going to look under the driver's seat?"

She gives me that look.

Anyway, she gets out of the car and opens the driver's side rear passenger door. She reaches under the seat. Well, look at that. There's a ball under the seat but that can't possibly make a beep beep noise. But, right next to it is a glass jar of blueberry jam with a metal top.

"You're kidding me? You are one fucking genius."

"Well, isn't that the reason why you married me?"

US Postal Service Change of Address Form

To put this into perspective, my wife and I are snowbirds. We live in NY during the spring and summer and part of the fall. We live in Florida for the Winter. Pretty simple, right?

Every year we need to inform the US Post Office of our Change of Address. Also pretty simple, right?

But, if you're like me, any and all government forms are never simple. They seem to ask questions that are vague and arbitrary. And they leave you totally confused.

Let's get started.

To complete the on-line form you will need a valid credit card and an e-mail address. We will charge you $1.10 for this service. So, how did you come up with the dollar and ten cent charge? And, "If you prefer not to use your credit card, you can fill out PS Form 3575 acquired from your local Post Office." But, do I want to go to the post office and wait in line for an hour to save a dollar and ten cents?

Followed by: "Note: The person who prepares this form states that he or she is the person, executor, guardian, authorized officer, or agent of the person for whom mail would be forwarded under this order. Anyone submitting false or inaccurate information on this form is subject to punishment by fine or imprisonment or both under Sections 2, 1001, 1702 and 1708 of Title 18, United States Code."

Holy cow! I'm just changing my mailing address and you're threatening me with jail time?

Who's moving? Individual or family? Well, what if some of the family is moving and some are not? What constitutes a family? What about my dog? She gets mail sometimes. What if we all have different names?

What type of move is this? Permanent or Temporary. Now, there's a question for you! What's permanent? What's temporary? If I move for more than 6 months is it permanent? When I decide to return, is that also permanent? So you can see, I'm only on the first page of this form and I'm already stuck.

When should we start forwarding your mail? *Hmmmm.* If I told you starting tomorrow, wouldn't some of my mail end up sitting in my mailbox until I returned in 6 months? And if I told you two weeks in advance, wouldn't you start forwarding my mail immediately? How do I know which day is the best day to tell you? Is it simply an arbitrary decision by a clerk at the local post office?

What's your old address? That's an excellent question! But, does that mean where I used to live, where I am living, or where I grew up in the 1940s?

And, don't get me started on "what's my new address?"

Can I have my mail forwarded to a hospital, a prison, a public park restroom, a Cuban restaurant, my hair salon, McDonald's? Can you forward my mother's chocolate cookies to my military address in central Somalia?

Okay, I somehow figured out how to complete the form and then...before I can hit 'FINISH" you ask me if I want discount coupons to stores I never heard of. And you won't let me leave your site until I answer all of these stupid questions?

Are you planning to buy a bed, a house, a horse or. an odd lot of lumber?

Will you allow us to send you a myriad of coupons like you get from CVS (enough to keep you warm around your shoulders in a rough winter storm)?

Too Much, Too Little, Too Expensive

I think you could call this my Andy Rooney rant. For those of you who don't remember him, Andy was the curmudgeon opinion commentator on CBS "60 Minutes" from 1969-2011.

"Rooney typically offered satire on trivial everyday issues such as the cost of groceries, annoying relatives, or faulty Christmas presents. Rooney's appearances on 'A Few Minutes with Andy Rooney' often included whimsical lists, such as types of milk, bottled water brands, car brands, and sports mascots."

WIKIPEDIA

My rant includes subjects that annoy me in 2023. Although I must say that many of my rants cover a similar territory as Andy's. Maybe we share the same parents. Although I think that would have been a medical miracle.

Back in the day (whenever that was), we seemed to have more of just about everything we bought at the store. For example there are air freshener aerosol cans. My mother used to put a can in the bathroom, and it seemed to last about ten years. Now, maybe we sprayed less back then. Or maybe we ate different foods that didn't deliver the same lingering...you know .... odor. But these days, a can of this stuff seems to last about two weeks. So, are the manufacturers filling the cans with less anti-smell stuff? Or, are we using more? The jury is out.

It's the same issue with a small box of tissues. Back in the day, these boxes seemed to last on the bedside table for at least a few months.

Today? Maybe there are 12 tissues in each box. And, I don't know about you, but I sneeze a lot more than I used to. So I go through a box in a week. That's probably about 75 cents a tissue. Maybe I should start using the other side? Oh, come on, it's only a sneeze.

Have you been dining at any fancy restaurants lately? I mean the really fancy ones where appetizers start at $30 each and entrees start at $60 per plate. Have you noticed that the descriptions are more wordy and filled with language that you have to look up on Google? Well, it seems to me that the wordier the menu description, the smaller the entree. I'm sorry, but I didn't expect my grilled salmon to be the size of an aspirin, or the lamb chops to be the size of a George Washington Quarter. The only thing that's large in these restaurants is the bill. That is a big bite out of your wallet.

And then there's too much stuff. Let's start with your television. Do you really watch the shows on 265 stations? Wrestling in Spanish? How to properly pluck a pigeon on the Food Network? The debates at a City Council Meeting in Intercourse, Pennsylvania? Just keep flipping through the stations you'll soon discover you watch about five stations. And, maybe a movie channel. Although I can do without The Texas Chainsaw Massacre.

Now let's go shopping at one of the big box stores like Costco. "Now honey, we only need some cheese, a few vegetables and a loaf of bread." Sounds good. Let's start with lane 1. Maybe I need a new diamond ring or a gold watch or a new computer or a 120" large screen TV? Well, those aisles will surely break the bank before you even get started shopping. How 'bout a 25 lb box of laundry detergent? Or, a 120-piece set of Allen Wrenches? Look, let's just get that 35 lb of American cheese, 12 loaves of bread, and a 50 lb. case of cherries and get out of here.

I love barbecued ribs. So we went to our favorite barbecue restaurant. I'm confronted with a choice: a half rack or a whole rack. Do I have a clue what size the cow was? Will my order fit on a plate, platter, or kitchen pan? Is there enough room on the table for my order? What do I do with the bones and my greasy fingers? A fella's got to know what he's getting into these days.

Cars are large and expensive. Houses are, too. Even jet fighters cost millions of buckaroonies. And, don't get me started on lawyers, eggs, hamburgers and nuts.

So, that's where I leave this. It all makes me nuts.

Costco

"Hey, honey. I think we need to go shopping at Costco. I need a package of pistachios and some lettuce."

"Okay that sounds like a good idea."

Two things. Two minutes. Twenty bucks. What could go wrong? Every time we decide to go shopping at Costco, we clean out our wallets. A minimum of $200.

"Oh, look at that, they have a five pack of weirdo vegetable chips."

"Wow, look at the great price on that 16 carat ring"

You know I really need a pair of pliers. Here's a 97 piece tool set. I think I see a pair of pliers in that package. Didn't you need some laundry detergent? Here's 62 lb. box for only 168 dollars.

Let's go over to the food section to pick up that lettuce. Look at those seedless grapes–20 lbs. For $44. And apples…a box of 50 for $66.

I think I'll take a taste of their organic orange juice. Yum. Let's buy twelve 84-ounce containers.

Take a look at that side of beef. 275 lbs…we could probably fit that in our freezer, right. We can cut it up into 35-lb steaks.

We get onto the checkout line. How is it possible that the guy in front of me has 192 boxes of Juicy Juice and 40 sacks of baking potatoes. And his credit card isn't working.

Okay, let's get checked out and head to the car. Wait a minute. Where's the lettuce and pistachios?

Sephardic Wedding

"What are you doing on Saturday night?"
"I dunno."
"Ya wanna make some money?"
"Sure. What's the deal?"
"There's a wedding at the Sephardic Temple. They need Busboys. And it's a BYOB event."
"What's BYOB?"
"Bring your own bottle. It should be fun."
"Okay, I'll see you there."

It was 1962, I was 15. Being a busboy was pretty easy work. The couple gets married. They eat. We clean up. I'm guessing everyone was gone by about 11:00 PM. The busboys were the only ones left in the synagogue. We finished the clean up and looked at what was sitting on each table: booze. I'd never seen so much booze. We looked around and realized that the guests left the booze and went home. So what were a group of 15 year old boys supposed to do? We each grabbed a bottle and proceeded to drink. I grabbed the bottle marked J&B. It was mostly full.

Since I had very little experience with alcohol (other than Manischewitz Wine on Passover), I thought I should give it a try. "Hey let's go bowling."

"Yeah, that sounds like fun."

As we walked to the bowling alley I took a swig...and another. And another and another. We arrived at the bowling alley and I took a final swig. I'd say I took a good stab at drinking the bottle dry.

We traded out our shoes for bowling shoes and walked over to the lane. I picked up a ball and slid down the alley as I threw the ball with all of my power down the lane. A strike. No, wait. Two strikes. Well, it sure looked that way. Two sets of pins all went down at once. I turned around and fell over the ball return. And that's all I remember.

The next day I was told my friend carried my body home. My mother answered the door. "Is he dead?"

"No, Mrs. Silverman. I think he just had too much to drink."

They carried my seemingly lifeless body to my bed and tossed me into it. I slept through the night and half of the next day. *Hmmm....* J&B ... maybe not the best choice. Maybe I should try Southern Comfort next time around?

I Used To

I used to read *The New York Times*.

From cover to cover. The world news...the national news...and the local news. I loved turning the bulky pages and folding that whale of a newspaper.

I used to read *Newsday*. It was the only Long Island newspaper that opened like a book. And it was all ads. Well, 90% ads, 6% high school sports, and 4% news. I had no interest in high school sports.

I used to ride my bike every day...to deliver newspapers and to feel the wind in my hair. Now that was exhilarating!

I used to go to school everyday and dream about romping on the beach with that hot English teacher.

I used to work at one of those boardwalk games, dreaming about eating dinner at that tiny Italian restaurant that made the best meatballs and spaghetti sauce you could ever imagine.

I used to body surf in the ocean. Those were the best cheap thrills that money couldn't buy.

I used to study the centerfold pictures in each month's *Playboy* magazine. I almost wanted to become a professional photographer from that kind of exposure.

Because you can't become good at something like that until you study it carefully and in-depth.

I used to date a girl in San Francisco. She had plans to blow up a TV tower. Well, the sex was great.

I used to smoke pot and look at the world through rose-colored glasses.

I used to go to parties and play "Spin the Bottle," so I could figure out how to get to 2nd base.

I used to have a girlfriend who liked to argue. I don't remember the arguments but boy did she have wonderful curves.

I used to jump from the top step at the 6th floor down 10 steps at a time to see how fast I could reach the ground floor.

I used to ride on the side of a refrigerator carton down a snowy hill.

I used to ride a motorcycle in and around NYC until I fell off of it…twice.

I once bought a car for $400 in Cleveland. I drove it to the top of a hill. The engine exploded. I couldn't stop laughing.

I once hitchhiked in the Rocky Mountains. An underaged kid was driving along the crazy curves at 80 miles an hour. I'm glad to report we arrived in Aspen in one piece.

I used to run like the wind on the first beach day into the ocean and fall flat on my stomach.

I used to smoke Camel Cigarettes like I was a big shot.

I used to do a lot of crazy things. I wish I still did.

An Imprecise Guy Living in a Precise World

As far as I'm concerned, there are two kinds of people in the world: those who are precise and those who are not precise. The precise people always need to know exact information: what, where, when, how and how much? Those who are imprecise just need a general idea that they should always bring their glasses, make sure their socks are on the right feet, and be sure to pull up their pants.

The precise people can't function without defined boundaries. They need to know where the fence line is, where the gate is, where the lock is and where the boss is. Further, they need to know what time dinner is, what's for dinner, where they will be fed and who's bringing the Maker's Mark whiskey.

Imprecise people only need a folding chair. Preferably one that easily opens and closes so if necessary, they can make a quiet escape into the parking lot. Well, you know that too much information requires an escape plan.

Precise people are excellent listeners. They hear every word and they digest all of them. Facts feed their bingo card. Of course, if an important fact is missing, then their world goes off the skids. For example: "What do you mean that the meeting will start around 7 or 7:30?"

"I'm going to buy you a shirt. It will be kind of blue/gray."

"Dinner will include a side dish. I'm sure it will be some kind of vegetable."

Imprecise people generally go with the flow. They're more interested in the big picture. A meeting? Whenever is fine. A blue/gray shirt? That's the perfect color. Dinner? That would be great.

I call imprecise people generalists. They hear spoken language like you would read Cliff Notes. Instead of reading: "It was a dark and spooky night along the Thames River in the center of London with nary a soul on the street. A sexy woman passed by and glanced at me. I was both scared and curious." A generalist would hear: "Someone took a walk in London at night. It could have been an exciting moment. But it was just weird." The generalist always got the gist of the scene but often misses out on the salacious details.

Generally speaking, women are more precise than men. For example: man says to woman: "George called. He said Billy was in an accident."

Woman Responds: "What happened?"

Man: "I dunno. George called. He said Bill was in an accident."

Woman to Man: "Was he hurt?"

Man to Woman: "I dunno. George called. He said Bill was in an accident."

Woman to Man: "Well, where is Billy?"

Man to Woman: "I dunno. George called. He said Billy was in an accident."

Precise people go to the supermarket with a list: Milk, eggs, bread, cheese... Imprecise people walk into the supermarket and just see what's in front of their nose. Four pounds of lightly salted butter. Buy 10 bars, get one free. Day old bread. Take two and we'll give you three. Cream cheese. Buy a 4 pound tub and we'll throw in a spreader.

Generally speaking, I'm an imprecise kind of guy. I married a very precise gal. They do say that opposites attract. It's probably true and quite amazing. Over the years we've figured out how to fill in the blanks for each other. And, sometimes, go blank in front of each other. "What are you talking about?"

"Oh, nothing."

How I earned a graduate degree from New York University, landed a job at Virginia Commonwealth University, and operated my own film production business must have something to do with smoke and mirrors.

Wellcare

"Thank you for calling Wellcare. If you are trying to reach One Care, We Care, Some Care, Who Cares or, You're Kidding Me Pharmaceuticals, Press 1. If you're trying to reach We Care, You Think We Care, We Used To Care, or, I'd Like to Think You Care, Press 2."

[BEEP]

You have reached the Wellcare Help Line. We're here to help you, guide you, steer you, and help find you the help that you need. But, first we need to confirm who you are exactly. Please enter your date of birth. No, that's wrong. You need to enter the month, day and year you were born. No, that's wrong. Don't you know when you were born? Didn't you attend your birthing session? You need to enter the month using three letters. If you don't know the third letter you're just dumb and we can't help you. If you know the day you were born speak clearly into your phone. No, you couldn't have been born on the 32nd of the month. Okay, just tell us the year you were born. No, we don't believe you were born in the 1400s, Just go back and get this shit straight.

No, let us know your Member Number. If you need 5 seconds, we can wait until you dig up your wallet and dig past your Gentleman's Club cards, Jiffy Lube, Victoria's Secret and Greasy Spoon Diner cards. No, your number is not YouSuck123. Try again.

Now, in a few simple words, let us know why you are calling.
"I need to .."
"I'm sorry, I did not get that. Try again."
"I have a ..."
"I'm sorry, I did not get that."
"In less than a few words tell us how we can help you."

"I want to …"

"I'm sorry. We are experiencing a great deal of incoming calls and you will have to wait 16 hours before we can connect you with an operator." Do you have a Tesla battery that you can keep connected during this time? Please stay on the line. If you hang up, you'll need to start this process all over and the wait time might be six weeks.

[PAUSE]

"Hello, my name is Nakeesh Schwandarama. Can you tell me your date of birth? I do not understand you. Can you say it like you grew up in Brooklyn? Okay. And, now I need your Social Security Card Number."

"I don't want to give you my Social Security Number."

"Okay, what was your Great Great Great Grandmother's nickname?"

"Bubblelah."

"Okay."

"That's good. Now, what can I help you with?"

"I ordered six drugs for renewal five weeks ago. I haven't seen a confirmation nor have I received any drugs since my order."

"Okay. Let me look up your files. Tell me your last name."

"Silverman."

"Silverwond?"

"No, Silverman."

"Sliverwound?"

"No, Silverman."

"Can you spell your last name?"

"S-I-L-V-E-R-M-A-N"

"I'm sorry. You seem to be breaking up. Can you do that again? Okay, got it."

"I see you tried to order Hydrocorotriamyasimey, is that correct?"

"No. It's Hydrocordomyasin."

"Can you spell that?"

"No."

"Can you spell 'encyclopedia?' If you can't just look it up Jimmeney Crickett on Google. He did a great rendition on the Mickey Mouse Club in the 1950s."

"What's the next drug on your list?"

"Xeralto."

"Do you spell that Zereltdo?"

"No."

"Do you spell that Zeer-L-toe?"

"No."

"Would you like me to spell it in Tamil (the language of Sri Lanka)."

"Yes. That would be helpful."

"Okay. Let me go to Google Translate. I'm sure they will scramble the spelling much worse that I did."

"Do you have any other drugs you would like to renew?"

"Yes."

"Can you tell me which ones?"

"I'm afraid to."

"Maybe I'll just go into CVS and wait in line for two weeks. They are always reliable enough to tell me that the drugs are on backorder and I'll have to pay $35,000 more than my pharmaceutical coverage allows. That's always comforting."

"Wellcare. You guys nailed it with that name."

Smoking Pot

We were on our Honeymoon traveling from Rome to Brindisi. We just finished our incredible adventure from England to France, Amsterdam, Germany, Spain and Italy. It was a two-and-a-half month whirlwind backpack tour to see the sights and sounds and taste the
flavors of Europe.

We were on a train using what was left of our Eurail Pass. The train was filled to the brim with travelers...mostly locals and a few tourists. Since Mary Anne spoke some Italian she got a seat among some local women. They were chatting up a storm and eating the lunch they brought with them. One was eating some really stinky cheese. The other was coursing down a can of anchovies. Oh, I thought...this is gonna be a long and memorable trip.

I was standing in the vestibule minding my own business. There was a kind of swarthy-looking guy standing next to me. We both had long hair (which in 1971 was generally assumed to be a sign of common interests in music and popular culture).

He was smoking a joint. And, after a few puffs he offered to share his inebriant with me. I willingly participated. I'm not sure how long we stood In the vestibule but, now that I look back at a map on Google, the train ride was just short of six hours. To me it seemed like about an hour. I guess it was some pretty good pot.

John was a Brit. He grew up in the southwestern England area. That's all I remember about his personal history. I'm guessing our conversation was mostly of a gestalt nature...where are you heading? Why do you know about Greece? Do you speak any Greek? Where will you stay when you get there? Etc., etc.

John didn't seem to have any set plans and neither did we. It was a really interesting two and half months of travel. No set plans. No Reservations. We camped on a hillside, along a river's back, on a mountaintop...it didn't matter. Well actually, we might have had a plan to set up our tent at a campsite on Brindisi. John followed us. We spent a few Nights at this place. I don't remember much except that a bottle of Retsina...Greek wine was five Dramas equal to $2.15 in US dollars. Let's just say that we consumed quite a bit of Retsina over the next few days.

In the campsite we met up with a few other wayward travelers. Two blonde girls from Silver Spring, Maryland. They were the type who finished each other's sentences. Always entertaining.

All of a sudden our twosome was now a foursome. Nobody had a plan or agenda. We just wanted to travel and have some fun.

As I recall, our group grew to seven or eight. We moved onto Athens and then to camping on the beach on the Island of Syros. Ah, Syros. Somebody at the American Express told us about this island. You take the boat from Athens and land into the Port of Syros. Then you take a bus to the far end of the island. But, wait... we landed around midnight. No bus. No hotel. Just a sleepy little port town. What are a bunch of weary innocent travelers to do? John went for a walk and about 10 minutes later came back riding on the back of a small truck. He met a Church Sexton who was deaf. But, that didn't matter because none of us spoke Greek. He waved us over to his living quarters that were cut into a stone outcropping. He brought out a lantern and pointed to the stone patio suggesting we camp out there for the night. He even brought us some wine. We spent the night under the stars. It was glorious. The next morning we met his sister who spoke some English. We asked her to thank her brother and we set out for the morning bus.

Just as it was described, we rode the bus to the other side of the mountain. Got off the bus. Walked around the peak of.a small mountain and there it was: a lovely beach, with figs you could pick off of the trees and a wonderful nude beach. We spent a few days there fishing, cooking and frolicking around. And then we headed home.

I think John's last name was Rolfe.

Maybe he was a descendant of the famous Brit John Rolfe, who was credited with exporting tobacco. Pot? Tobacco? Wouldn't that be ironic?

John visited us years later when we lived on Staten Island. It felt like time had never passed. Still Gestalt. But that was the last time we ever saw him.

Trust

Thoughts and phrases found on the internet:

"To believe that someone is good and honest and will not harm you, or that something is safe and reliable."

"I knew that wasn't a good deal. I should never have trusted her."

"Oh, I trust you .....I trust you as far as I can throw you."

Loan broker : "Oh, don't get me wrong. I trust you. We trust all our customers. Why, this bank was *built* on trust. Here. Sign here."

Loan broker : "Uh, you gotta get closer. This pen is chained down, you know."

And, one of my all time favorites...

(Billboard advertising Irving Trust Bank in NYC).

"Our last name is Trust, but you can call us Irving"

"Trust me, this won't hurt a bit. *OUCH!* Well, it didn't hurt the last guy. And, he didn't even trust me."

"Trust me when I say I'll be at the meeting on time."

"When others say, 'Trust me!' in this sense, we are being asked to believe their character, circumstances, capability, resources and behavior are dependable/reliable."

"Trust is the cornerstone of business. It's the basis of every human relationship, every interaction, every communication, every initiative, every work project and even any strategic imperative you need to accomplish. Trust is essential. Without it, social groups can't function properly."

"When you can't believe your eyes, you can always trust your heart."

"When you're choosing a used car, You can trust me on this one."

"Trust is like the air we breathe – when it's present, nobody really notices; when it's absent, everybody notices."

WARREN BUFFET

"Me? I'm dishonest and you can always trust a dishonest man to be dishonest. Honestly, it's the honest ones you have to watch out for."

CAPTAIN JACK SPARROW

Some years ago one of my clients needed a video to show at their annual shareholder's meeting. "What's the topic?"

"They need to know that our customers trust us."

"Do they...trust you? Can they trust you? How can you tell if they trust you?"

Stand them up. Close their eyes and push them backwards. If they don't scream, then it means that they trust you. And, if they do scream? Find another customer.

"To be trusted is a greater compliment than being loved."

"Trust me. You won't get pregnant this time."

"Trust me. You won't fall."

"Trust me. This ladder is safe."

"Trust me. I wouldn't poison you."

"Trust the water we drink, the cheese is not rancid, the milk is still good."

"Trust that the house won't fall down, the car will keep going, the pothole isn't too deep."

"Everything we do involves trust."

What's in a Name?

A few years back I was browsing the entertainment section of the New York Times. I wasn't looking for anything specific, probably because I'm such a neophyte. I didn't grow up in a house that played any kind of music, and that music appreciation class in college bored me to death. I think I remember hearing Jewish holiday songs and an occasional Kate Smith or Ethel Merman TV show where they belted out, "God Bless America" or "Everything's Coming Up Roses". I even remember Dinah Shore crooning the music for Chevrolet ("See the USA in Your Chevrolet"). And, I think I remember watching Liberace on the Ed Sullivan Show. But that was pretty much it.

But, back to the NY Times...my eye caught an article about Jeff Goldblum. For some odd reason, and I do mean "odd...I really like Jeff's acting style. I'm weird and quirky and he's weird and quirky. I guess you'd say he could easily be my brother from another mother doppelganger. Except we don't really look alike. In any case, the article announced Jeff's newest venture. He was going to perform with his Jazz Group in the lounge at New York's Carlyle Hotel.

Someone must have heard his group perform and decided that he would be a perfect fit for their upscale-but-ever-so-slightly-quirky audience. But there was one problem: the person who was charged with promoting the performance called Jeff and asked him what he called his group. Jeff was a bit perplexed. He never really thought about giving the group a name. "But, how will we promote you without a name?" she asked. He thought for a moment and said something like, "Oh, okay. We'll call ourselves "The Mildred Snitzler Orchestra." That made me laugh .. big time. Jeff said that Mildred was a friend of his mothers. She lived to be 100. Hey, why not name the group after her? Everyone needs fifteen minutes of fame. And so they continue to play great jazz as The Mildred Snitzler Orchestra.

It wasn't a big leap for me to start the wheels churning in my mind. "Hey, do you remember Mom's best friend from Forest Hills? Nelda Zelenko. I think she played canasta and seemed to show up at all of the holiday parties in our apartment. I can't recall if she was married, divorced, widowed or just one of those anomalies that crosses your life path every few centuries.

Nelda had a name that seemed to sound like an Iambic pentameter (For those who forgot the definition, here's the latest from Oxford's Dictionary; "a line of verse with five metrical feet, each consisting of one short (or unstressed) syllable followed by one long (or stressed) syllable"). Well, okay, it didn't quite fit that definition, but the thought made me laugh long and hard.

Nelda's name triggered another story about another name. I had a friend who lived on Staten Island. Like most people who found their way to our sweet country, his grandparents found their way to Ellis Island. They didn't speak a word of English. But, soon they found themselves standing in front of a US Immigration Officer: "Name?" he said. "Chamoodiz", the grandpa said. The Immigration Officer paused for just a moment and said, "Shapiro, step forward". It's really amazing what ignorance can do to your identity.

And, then a few other unusual names were triggered from my memory. There was Melvin Pozwolsky (a sweet spirited cherubic fellow in my high school class) and Siobhan Lubieniecka (who didn't look anything like her name. She was skinny as a rail with a sexy and infectious laugh). She was an occasional overnighter at our college crash pad. There was Moses Moses (we called him "Mo") and Joe Josephs and Billy Crystal (you know him, right?). And Richard Riddlebarger (we called him, "Dicky")

Then again, what's in a name?

Silverman Productions

For a guy who spent most of his professional career in the film production business (31 years), you'd think I'd have a few opinions about movies. Well, I do and I don't. I know a bit about how they are made, how to cast actors, how to build sets, scout locations, choose the right equipment, to know exactly how important the sound guy is, editing, etc., etc.

More importantly, I know when a script is well thought out and a story is well told. I know something about directing and producing and choosing the right crew. But anybody can know about all of that. There are plenty of books on those subjects.

I produced plenty of award-winning TV spots and corporate and public relations films. So, you'd think I would be a true cinephile. Yet, I'm not. I'm much more like your average movie goer. Well, except if it's a lousy movie. Then all I see are the continuity and editing mistakes. "Watch that guy eating a sandwich. First you see him take a first bite. Next, shot he's almost done. And, the third shot he's only taken two bites."

"Oh, and that cigarette ... first he lights it, next the ash is ⅔ down the shaft and then, it looks like he hasn't taken a single drag."

"And, look at that coffee mug. There's not a drop of liquid in there. What a fake sip that is."

I do like certain kinds of movies–particularly human interest stories like *Captain Fantastic* – a movie with a title that completely fools you– and *Midnight Run*–Charles Groden's dry sense of humor is simply wonderful– and *Little Miss Sunshine*–well, it was human and it had some interest.

I like movies that make me laugh (*Elvis and Nixon*– when my wife burst out into uncontrollable laughter at least three times I knew this film was truly funny– and *It's a Mad, Mad, Mad, Mad World*–I don't remember much about this movie because I was trying my best to put my arm around my high school date. My heart was pumping like a puppy's heart when my hand reached her right shoulder and…for crying out loud…it fell asleep…on her breast –so, I got smacked, and worst of all, my hand was numb so I didn't feel a thing). What was that movie I was talking about?

I also like films that make me cry (*Schindler's List, Shawshank Redemption*) And, I like time-tested films like *To Kill a Mockingbird* and *It's a Wonderful Life, The Birdman of Alcatraz* and *Twelve Angry Men*–this film might actually be my favorite.

I don't like many animated films, sci-fi or films with gratuitous violence.

Now, I must admit I have a few other issues that affect my movie going experience. I have a touch of sleep apnea added to my attention deficit disorder. In short, I often fall asleep when I'm watching a movie and, even if I watched the whole movie, I often forget what it's all about. Of course, if I liked it, I'll watch it again–even if I start in the middle–to try and tie the whole story together. It's a strange way to watch a film, but it's my way.

If I Could Fly

When I was 9, I was sure I had a magic power. I lived on the 6th floor of an apartment building in Forest Hills, Queens. One day, for no particular reason, I decided to walk downstairs to the lobby.

I don't think this was the first time for this event. I seemed to recall that I liked taking the stairs. Maybe it allowed me the opportunity to burn off some pent up energy. Or, maybe I hated being cooped up in an elevator. Or, maybe I discovered a game that didn't require any rules or competition, yet gave me a ton of self satisfaction.

I was sure I had a natural ability akin to a fast moving tap dancer. While I didn't know Fred Astaire, Gregory Hines, or Bill "Bojangles" Robinson, I was sure I had what they had: a natural ability to make my feet go clickety-clack.

Maybe it started out as a self-imposed race (though I didn't own a watch)? Maybe it was just a made-up kids' game? But I was compelled to fly down those six flights of stairs, and it wasn't just fast-walking or a game of skipping. It was an innocent, untrained dance. And boy did I look forward to flying down those stairs!

It all started very innocently. First, I started walking. One foot in front of the other...over time, it changed from a mean-to-an-end into a very fun way to get from A to B. Hey, I was a kid. If I was going to make it down 6 flights it needed to become a game. So I stepped up the pace. I started skipping some steps. First it was two or four leaps, and then I took a big leap and finished the flight in one grand jump!

After doing this for a time, I realized that when I landed on the hard floor my ankles and feet started to hurt. Clearly, it was time to change up the game. That's when a Eureka moment happened to me. It's time to try out my "slickedly-click" technique. One foot in front of the other. Toe first, heel follows. Slickedly-click. Since the stairs were made of stone, the sound was easily amplified.

The pace, technique and sound became intoxicating. I know this must sound ridiculous, but this "dance" was very satisfying. It not only gave me a great sense of accomplishment, but one of euphoria.

I don't recall how long this game went on—a week, a month or more. But it's a sweet memory between me, myself, and I. And I'll never forget it.

The Small Print

There are downsides to getting older. Your joints start to creak. Your memory starts to fade. And your eyes start to go.

Advertisers understand this dilemma all too well. I'm sure you've noticed the "mice print" in TV spots? You know what I'm talking about: TV commercials requiring more accurate details to clarify the "behind-the-gimmick pitch." Most often you see it in automotive, insurance, pharmaceutical, banking, and products or services requiring that you sign a contract like phone or internet services.

You also see this "fine print" (yet another name for it) in newspaper ads. But the TV spots are the most annoying. It's simply impossible to read the "mice type" in two seconds. You would need to have graduated *summa cum laude* from Dale Carnegie's speed reading class. And even then, your brain just couldn't grasp all those eenie weenie words.

According to Wikipedia: Fine print is controversial because of its deceptive nature. Its purpose is to make the consumer believe that the offer is really great. Though the real truth about the offer is "technically" available to the consumer in the smaller print of the advertisement—thus virtually ensuring plausible deniability from claims of fraud—it is often designed to be overlooked.

"Plausible deniability." I just love that expression. If it isn't already, it should be a classic oxymoron.

Which brings me to a very naïve question: Do advertisers really have to lie to us in order to sell us their wares? Are their products that lousy?

In an era where we distrust our elected officials and CEOs, you'd think an advertiser would want to step up to the plate and present a "squeaky clean" image. Procter & Gamble seems to have done a pretty good job. And so has Starbucks. (Although their coffee is pricey, it is what they say it is: a cup of coffee).

Bigger, Bigger, Big Tush Lottery

"Hey Honey..."

"Yeah...."

"Did you know that the Bigger, Bigger, Macho Bigger Florida Big Tush Lottery is up to $300 Billion Dollars?"

"Yeah...."

"Well, don't you think we should buy a ticket?"

"Yeah...."

"It's only two dollars."

"Yeah ... but, don't we have to drive somewhere to buy one?"

"We do."

"I dunno. That's a lot of work...getting up...getting dressed...putting on my shoes...driving to a store and then I have to decide if I should pick the numbers, or, let their machine pick the numbers...it's sooooooo much work....."

"Yeah ... but, $300 Billion is a pretty good payout even if the government takes $275 Billion for taxes. We could pay off our Off Track Betting Debt with that kind of payout."

"Yeah..."

"So...do you want to go out and buy a ticket?"

"What's the weather like?"

"It's raining hard...it's cold and very, very windy."

"Yeah ... well, you know you have to suffer if you're going to win the lottery."

"Who said that?"

"I dunno."

"Okay, let's go."

At the store

"Hi, I'm here to buy a lottery ticket."

"Okay, how many do you want?"

"Just one."

"Which lottery?"

"The Bigger, Bigger, Macho Bigger Florida Big Tush Lottery."

"The Mega Tush or the Power Tush?"

"The Bigger Bigger Bigger One."

"Okay. You got some numbers?"

"No. Just let the machine do it".

"Okay. Do you want to add the Bigger Bigger Multiplier Bigger that can add another $300 Billion to your Winnings? It's only another two dollars."

"Sure. Another $300 Billion could let us buy Mar-a-Lago. Or not. Maybe it's valued a little higher."

Back home

"Will you look at that ticket? Pink and long and filled with lots of black numbers and codes and rules and stuff."

"It says 'Big Tush' at the top. It shows the date and the day, and it says there are even more ways to suck you into upgrading your ticket. What a frickin' deal!"

"And on the left side of the ticket, there's a strip of hot pink that bleeds right into the rest of the ticket. You can just see the *BILLIONS* oozing over your numbers and running off the table."

"Honey, we need the Big Tush Mop to clean up this mess. We don't want our neighbors to come over and see all of these billions all over the floor."

"Well, they don't draw the winning numbers until 11:00 PM tonight. So, what do we do until then? We dream."

"If we win we can give a billion to the kids, a billion to the dog, a billion to the mailman, and the Amazon man, and the plumber. We can make contributions to the Help Everyone Fund, and the Save the World Fund, and the Be Nice to Your Dog Fund."

"We can buy a house bigger than the one that Bill Gates lives in, and a car that's smarter than the Tesla. And, we can buy an airplane that flies us anywhere and everywhere whenever and wherever we want to go."

"And maybe a self-cleaning bathroom."

"We could buy a shopper and a cook and a restaurant at every nook."

"And maybe we could buy the services of a psychiatrist who can help us figure out who our friends are and who just wants money."

"Hey, it's 11:00 PM."

"And the numbers are.........."

"Well maybe we can buy another ticket for next week's drawing."

Arm Sex

I'm fortunate that my wife takes care of all of our travel arrangements. She researches flights, car rentals, things to do, and places to see. She diligently looks for the best deals and the best travel packages.

She even looks for the best seats on a plane. She likes the window and I usually like the aisle. And all of that sort of stuff works out just fine. Except for this one flight—a few months ago—from LaGuardia to West Palm Beach.

Everything was going along pretty well. We arrived at the airport a few hours before boarding. We made our way to the gate. Grabbed a cup of coffee and we waited for the flight agent to announce when we were going to board the plane.

The announcement came and we got on line. I think we had seats about two thirds of the way towards the back of the plane. We headed down the gangway (if that's what's called) and found our seats. We lifted our carry-on luggage above our seats and proceeded to sit down. It turns out this time I had to sit in the middle seat. No big deal.

And then I wondered who would be sitting next to me. It turned out to be a big fella wearing a short-sleeved shirt. Of course, I'm also a big fella and I was wearing a short-sleeved shirt.

The plane took off. And it wasn't a moment before we were rubbing our hairy arms against each other. Thousands of little hairs soon became intimate friends. At first it seemed like we might have a truncated Mendelssohn Symphony about to happen. The hairs took their time getting to know each other. Then, my neighbor adjusted his arm and a long-lost wave of homecoming. It was like, "hey, I know you. You're the hairy arm I met last year on the flight to Denver."

Once I adjusted my arm, it seemed like a silent symphony began. Well not really, but, you get the idea.

As our arms went through their movements, so did the hairy symphony. At one point he decided to get up. I guess he thought it was intermission. But he was the only one in the aisle. After a bit, he sat down again. And so it continued. I'm convinced there must have been a conductor in the seat in front of us because we both started to perspire a little. The fine hairs were now performing in fake sync like Milli Vanilli from 1989.

I'd like to say this was a euphoric experience. But, that was just not the case. It turned into something akin to mud wrestling in an opera pit. When the conductor's wand went up...well... you can imagine what was going on.

Over the course of the flight he got up and he sat down. He got up and he sat down. Remember, he controlled the aisle.

Did my wife notice this symphony hall event in our aisle? Nah. She was deep into experiencing the fantasy of her romantic book. Our two-person Hairy Symphony missed her altogether, but I'm sure she got her share of brain sex.

Another day. Another flight on United Airlines.

(Isn't it ironic that we booked on United?)

Meatball War

If you're driving down Military Trail going south from Boynton Beach, it's easy to miss. The first turn in is just past the post office. If you miss that, the next one is just before you turn in for "The Girls." No, that's not a porn shop, but it sure sounds like one.

The goal is to find "The Boys." It's an oddball independent grocery. And it's been at that location for over 50 years. Considering the extreme competition for groceries in the area, it's quite a unique experience.

Of course, first you need to park your car. There are plenty of twists and turns with some parking right in front of the store. Then again, it's a challenge to maneuver between the customers going in-and-out and the drivers fighting for a spot. If you miss this opportunity, you'll need to weave in-and-out of the various lots around the store and maybe even wiggle in-between the trucks supplying fresh goods.

Once in, you're hit with a wall of food choices. Straight ahead are a wall of fresh apples. To the right, you enter into their sour pickles and smoked fish. The bakery is next, with an array of homemade birthday cakes, danishes, muffins, and fresh bread. Behind are the homemade spreads: lox and chives cream cheese, salmon and cream cheese, etc. A few steps further is their cheese shop. They will gladly cut you a piece of cheese from one of their big wheels of cheese: cheddar, manchego, stilton, French wine-infused cheese and many more wondrous choices.

Onto to their roasted coffees, fresh cut fruits and fresh squeezed juices. The meat counter is to the right and straight ahead is the hot bar of homemade foods.

As we pulled into the parking lot my wife asked me if I wanted anything special. I said a few of their homemade meatballs with their homemade red sauce would be wonderful. With that in mind, she began her trek. By the time she made it to the homemade food counter there was a woman who seemed to be buying up the store. "I'll have a pound of the chicken cacciatore, a pound of the sausages and peppers, two pounds of the pasta with bolognese sauce and so on. By this time another worker popped up behind the counter and asked my wife what she would like. She replied, "two meatballs with red sauce."

Meanwhile, the Big Order Lady had also requested two meatballs, ignoring my wife's order. Now, you need to know that there were only two meatballs left in the bin. My wife jumped in and said, I ordered them first. The Big Order Lady said they were for her son who was in the car. My Wife said, yeah, well those meatballs are for my husband who is also in the car with a fork and knife and napkin in hand. Just when both women were about to grab one of the meatballs and mush it into the other one's face, another woman behind the counter chimed in, "relax, we have more meatballs."

This infusion might have held off a Meatball War.

No boys stepped in. No girls stepped in. Just another day in the life of fighting for truth, justice and the American Meatball.

Southbound Subway

In the early '70s we lived on the north shore of Staten Island. For sure, it was a strange place to be if you were living in New York City. Few high rise buildings, one amazing hardware store, no hot dog stands, lousy Chinese food and no supermarkets nearby.

At first I was a full time student at New York University and Mary Anne was a Nurse. After I graduated, I got a job as the Program Director of the Staten Island Council of the Arts. Our connection to Manhattan was the Staten Island Ferry. For some odd reason on one particular day we decided to either see a Broadway show or to find some decent Chinese food for dinner. Or we did both. In either case, we knew that the Ferry ran once an hour during the late night hours. Wherever we were, it was about 11:00 PM and it was time to find our way to the #1 downtown express train. I think we were near 14th Street and that was one of it's stops. We made it over to the train, waited a while and then hopped onto one of the cars. As usual, the train pulled out of the station. We passed Houston, Canal, Franklin and Chambers Streets.

The doors closed and then there was an announcement. (jumbled, garbled, mumbo jumbo). The doors opened at Cortland St. The train pulled out of the station. We got to Rector Street. Another announcement (jumbled, garbled, mumbo jumbo). The doors did not open. The train proceeded. Well, we figured That stop must have been closed. The next stop was Cortland Street. I looked at Mary Anne and said, "I think This train is going backwards."

So, we got out and stepped onto the Platform. Nobody was there (after all it's the Wall Street area). There was a Transit Cop. So, we told him about the train that was going backwards. I even imitated the announcement with all of the gabled mumbo jumbo. He laughed. I didn't see what was so funny. He said that the Transit Authority is doing work at the South Ferry Station And you need to get off at Cortland St. Oh ... that was perfectly clear.

So, we got out and walked a few blocks but missed the midnight ferry. We did catch the 1:00 AM Ferry and soon realized that Mary Anne left her pocketbook on the subway. Good luck getting that back.

The next day MA's mother called her at the hospital where she worked and asked if she lost her pocketbook. Now, how did she know that? Some fine subway rider or another transit cop found it and turned it into Lost and Found.. Were her ID cards still in there? Yep. Was her money still in there? Yep.

New York, New York. It's a hell of a town. The Bronx is up and the Battery's down.

A Moment In Time

I guess it all started in 1973. It was a late afternoon on the North Shore of Staten Island. Not a particularly notable place. We lived upstairs in a two-family house just across from a gypsum factory and just across the Kill Van Kull from what I called "Gas/Oil New Jersey". I was waiting to start my graduate school program at New York University and, in the meantime, I was driving a taxi in Manhattan part-time at night. Also not a particularly notable job.

Mary Anne worked the 4:00 PM to midnight shift at a local hospital. She was an RN doing her best to help mankind recover through all kinds of surgeries and ailments. Her shift was about to begin. She had just put on her nurse's outfit and was ready to head for work.

I was in my mid-20s and she was just 20. I guess she saw that sparkle in my eye. Maybe it was her nurse's outfit that worked its magic on me. Oh, the pleasure of testosterone and youth. We looked at each other and, well let's just say her departure for work took a slightly-delayed turn of events. "But, honey I'm not on the pill and we're not using any protection," followed by my famous last words, "oh, don't worry...nothing is going to happen."

A few weeks later Mary Anne announced: "I'm pregnant."

"Oh," I said, "Well, how did that happen?"

She said, "Remember that afternoon a few weeks ago when you were drinking a 'Piel's Real Draft Beer?'"

"Yeah ... "

"And, I was wearing my nurse's white outfit."

"Yeah."

"Oh .. Oh .. you mean it's that easy to get pregnant?'

"Yeah ..."

"Well, what does this mean?"

"Duh .. we're going to have a baby."

"Really?"

"Well, I didn't know it was that easy to do this. I thought the odds were kind of high to make this thing happen."

"I'm Sicilian. Getting pregnant is easy for us."

Well, the next weeks turned into months, and Mary Anne's profile adjusted accordingly. We joined a Natural Childbirth class. "Natural" childbirth. Now there's an interesting thing. I had no idea why we needed to learn how to do something that was "natural". Anyway, we went to the classes. I think it was the second or third class when the teacher was teaching the soon-to-be mothers how to breathe.

"You need to learn how to "breathe?"

This was a new concept to me. Well, the teacher started to demonstrate breathing techniques when you go into labor. And, then she said, "if you learn this technique, delivering your baby won't hurt."

At which point I blurted out, "Bullshit!"

The teacher stopped, gave me a steely eyed stare and said, "Excuse me!"

Let's just say, I backed off.

The months passed. The belly expanded. And soon the day had come.

"Honey, I think we need to go to the hospital."

"Oh, okay. But, can I take a shower first? I'll be quick. Just hang in there." Probably the most insensitive thing I've ever said, especially since she was in labor since midnight.

We left for the hospital posthaste, checked in, and found ourselves in a private room.

"So, what do we do now?"

"We wait for the doctor and for me to dilate."

Then, it was time to happen. They moved us into a delivery room. Mary Anne's legs were lifted into some kind of device. We waited a while longer until the doctor arrived. He examined her and said, "it looks like it's about time to push. Donald, you stand here in front of Mary Anne and you'll be able to see the baby being born."

I can't remember what I said, but I guess I was compliant. Of course, I had no idea what was about to happen. The next thing I knew she was pushing. I must have been turning green, purple, gray...who knows what other colors. I'm sure I was about to faint. The doctor quickly grabbed me and parked my body behind Mary Anne's shoulders. He said, "STAY HERE!"

I compiled. And the baby was born...screaming and hollering and bloody and messy and there he was...Daniel Jay Silverman. Just like that.

Easy, right?

49 Years Later and Here We Are in Sun Valley East

I'm still amazed how our two lives align
the two of us! A pair! Take it as read,
old love, I thought I'd never see the time
The tangle of our jumpers in the line,
the battle for the blankets in our bed
confirm that I am yours, and you are mine.
So then, this is my pledge, my valentine:
my hand's in yours for all that lies ahead.
Oh love, there's never been a better time
now that I'm yours, and finally, you're mine.

All of My Friends are Quirky

I dunno. Maybe it's my age and that I'm afforded the opportunity to look back. Maybe it's because I'm kind of weird that I seem to attract weirdos. Maybe it's because I'm Jewish and everybody's Jewish mother was the dominating force in weirdness. Whatever the case, I'm seldomly surprised at just how weird my friends really are.

Take my friend Neil for example. Many years ago he introduced me to his theory of "all inanimate objects have their own distinct personalities". And, then he proceeded to tell me about his Volkswagen Bug car radio. For some odd reason, it didn't work *unless* you brought a wooden matchstick into the car. No, it didn't need to be threatened with fire. But, it did need to have the non-match side of the stick jammed into the left corner of the radio to make it work. I saw this demonstration with my own eyes. Once he jammed in the stick the damn thing worked.

Neil also had an old standup lamp that also required a matchstick in order to light up. Here...watch me, he said. Go figure?

My brother-in-law is more on the superstitious side. "If you don't want bad luck, make sure you turn your bath towel towards the wall when you hang it up." Guess what? This old wives' tale must have something to it because I can't start my day without hanging the bath towel just that way.

And then there was my friend Mitchell. We both grew up in a very Jewish neighborhood on Long Island. When the Jewish High Holidays approached (I think it was 1960), the World Series Games coincided with the holidays. And, as any follower of the High Holidays knows, you can't make a fire during this period because it is a symbol of work. Thus, any contemporary extension to fire making is also prohibited. So, if you wanted to watch the World Series you couldn't turn on the TV because it required a spark to start the TV. What did my friend Mitchell teach me? Buy yourself a "Shabbos Clock" otherwise known as a pre-set timer. Set the clock – the night before the holiday begins – to the time the World Series game starts. And, voilà! Now you are just watching the game without creating a fire. Wow. That's one quirky work-around idea.

Some of my friends have food quirks. Whenever I went to a restaurant with my friend Lee he would study the menu as if it was an engrossing murder mystery. It appeared as if he needed to interpret the menu selection to be sure that his familiar standards of a tasty meal were met. What do you mean it's roasted? Or braised? Or blackened? Wait a minute ... didn't my mother invent the word "blackened?" What's in the tuna fish salad? I don't like raw carrots or celery or any weird spices like dill weed. Oh, it's prepared like that? Make me a burger with a nice slice of Bermuda Onion.

I have another friend Joe who I meet for lunch a few times a year in NYC. He mostly wants to go to vegetarian restaurants because, "as you know, I only eat dirt". That means he's very particular about carefully ordering foods that are mostly natural. One time I talked him into going to a famous Ukranian restaurant on NYC's Lower East Side. It was busy and crowded and fast-paced. When the waiter approached he said, "okay boys, what'll it be?" Joe deferred to me first. I ordered a normal menu item just the way they described it. Then it was Joe's turn. He was ordering while he was reading the menu at the same time, "I'll have the eggwhite omelet..." and then Joe noticed there were a litany of vegetable options to add onto it. So, he said, and "add the yada yada yada." The waiter paused for a moment and said, "we don't have no yada yada yada." I burst out laughing.

My friend Jeff is in his own category altogether. He has a very limited palate. I don't think he ever boiled a pot of water in his life. He eats out every meal of the day. His routine is pretty regular: a burger, spaghetti, eggs and a bagel. Ask him about vegetables: "I don't eat broccoli, asparagus, or brussel sprouts. Never did. Never will. I dunno. I think my mother cooked them until they were dead."

And me? Oh, I'm normal. I don't walk under ladders. I hate kale. I hate wearing a tie. I pee in the shower. And I always turn the toilet paper face-down.

An Old Fart's Guide to Planet Earth

"Youth is wasted on the young."

GEORGE BERNARD SHAW

Some say there's a benefit to growing older. You see a lot. You hear a lot. You filter a lot more. If you're lucky, the superfluous stuff floats up to the top and you're left with the cream of wisdom. Or just a clogged drain.

In any case, there's a lot to be said about looking back at your many years to consider the best ideas you ignored.

We're overwhelmed by information: news, books, music, conspiracy theories, recipes, dog stories, bathroom gardening...you name it. As much as time allows, we absorb what we can. But, how do you know if you're using your precious time wisely? Do you know if the early information that you learned as a kid wasn't just perfect?

There was a time when we read using only one candle by the bed. The lighting was lousy. The smoke was unpleasant. When the candle burned out you needed to close your book. Hopefully, you had just enough time to read enough food for thought. As you were about to close your eyes you couldn't help but try to digest your reading.

Today, we read morning, noon and night and slather some TV over it all. But is there really much to digest with such a smorgasbord of information?

Another example: We drive...fast and mindlessly. To and from work, shopping, movies, takeout restaurants, to the locksmith and to FedEx. We seem to need to pack it all in as fast as possible. Fast is good...sometimes. We like fast internet service and a fast pregnancy (not that I would know anything personally about that). But maybe fast isn't so good. Maybe a return to the horse and buggy would do us justice. Maybe we should slow down to just one horsepower. Maybe getting to the destination quickly isn't the best objective?. Maybe the process of getting there is more satisfying? Did you ever change a flat on a horse and buggy? Did you ever listen to an Amish Rock and Roll Station while cruising at one mile and hour? There's no doubt in my mind that you'd surely learn all of the words.

Slowing down also means you will have time to learn lessons from the birds and the bees. Just sit and watch them doing their business. They go this way and that way and this way and then that way and on and on for a long time. They must have a plan. Or they just spend their days doing their mating dance for hours on end. As the Jackson Five sang, "It's easy as 1, 2, 3, or simple as Do-Re-Mi, A, B, C, 1, 2, 3, baby, you and me, girl!" Just think, you won't need to go to sex ed or childbirth classes anymore.

Enough of my silliness. Let's get moving.

Zumbaaaaaaaa.

Rockaway Playland

When I grew up in Long Beach, NY, summers were always something special. Of course it was warm outside, so I could fly out the door wearing just my shorts and t-shirt. I could ride my bike anywhere in the neighborhood. I could ride as fast as I wanted and let go of the handlebars to live a little dangerously. I could feel the wind in my hair. It was simply joyous. When I turned 11 or 12, I had a newspaper delivery route. While it sounded like work, it was actually a lot of fun.

A pack of newspapers was delivered to my garage everyday. I snipped the metal wire that kept it together and started to individually roll them so I could add a rubber band to hold it together. I stacked them into the front basket on my bike and was ready to start the delivery process. To me, it was a game. I rode my bike as fast as I could, flinging newspapers to the left and flinging newspapers to the right. One landed on a front step. Another landed on the front walk. Another landed on the wet grass. Oh, well. Better luck next time.

I had about 60 papers to deliver on my route. Every day was a fun adventure.

Somewhere during that period of time of my of life my Dad decided he wanted to take me out to visit Rockaway Playland. Rockaway Playland? A kid's dream come true. Rides, boardwalk games, cotton candy...what could be better? And alone, with just my dad. This never happened. My dad was an orphan. He had a very tough childhood. How he came out so kind and loving is truly amazing. A trip to the Playland with just my dad was wonderful in and of itself.

It was just a 20-minute drive to get there. Follow the road along the beach, go over the Atlantic Beach Bridge and drive a little bit farther.

It seemed to be a quiet afternoon at the Playland. I'd imagine this is the kind of place that gets cracking when the sun goes down. Anyway, it was all good for me. I can't recall the games that I played first. The water pistol game...the throw-the-ball-in-the-hole game...skee ball...who knows? I'm sure I was drunk with joy.

My very favorite ride was Bumper Cars. You paid some money and entered an enclosed arena filled with small metal cars that had big rubber bumpers. You got into the car and the ride operator told you, "now be sure not to bump the cars."

Yeah sure. He started the ride and I was Parnelli Jones. I banged this guy to the left and smashed into the girl on my right. I criss-crossed the arena and banged into anyone who was driving along minding their own business. Man oh man, I couldn't stop laughing. This ride was even more fun than flinging newspapers. I think I rode in a second session just to squeeze out more aggressive joy.

I remember getting off the ride with a huge smile on my face. My dad seemed to be happy that I was so happy. It was a great moment where we bonded. I would imagine he would have liked to ride in one of the bumper cars...if only he fit into one of them.

The next and last game I played was a simple coin toss. There was a 4x4 wooden block that was slickly painted white with colored circles all over it. The objective was to stand behind a barrier and toss a coin onto the block. If your coin fully landed into a circle you won a prize. I watched a few people give it a try. They just tossed a quarter onto the block. Just about all of them landed and slid off the slippery board and into a pit. Your quarter was gone forever. Anyway, I decided to take a different approach. I threw the quarter high up in the air.. so when it landed it wouldn't slide across the slippery board. My quarter went up and up and up and down and down and down and landed on the board. And, it slid...just a bit...and landed inside a colored circle. I jumped up and down screaming, "I WON...*I WON!*"

And it was true. The guy behind the counter grabbed the biggest stuffed teddy bear you've ever seen. It had to be three feet tall! It was such a thrilling moment for a kid. To this day I'm not sure if the big stuffed animal or the act of winning the game made my day. In any case, my Dad was happy and so was I. Surely a day to remember.

The Tooth Fairy

I don't really remember many things about my very early years except for one thing. I distinctly remember the Tooth Fairy. The arrangement was pretty straight forward: you lose a tooth, you put it under your pillow. You find money under your pillow in the morning. So, here was this innocent tooth. For as long as I could remember, it seemed to be doing a yeoman's job of chomping down on my Captain Crunch cereal in the morning and an equally good job of sawing through that concrete cookie/cracker my Aunt Anna called mandel bread. My tooth also managed to grind down Mom's extra crunchy kugel. Best .. or worst, of all...it always successfully got stuck in her honey and gooey *taiglach* (a small mountain of Jewish honey dough).

My sweet and innocent tooth seemed to work well for as many years as I could remember (being about 6 years old, I didn't have a long history). My little tooth had many uses. It added to my smile so I didn't look like a dork. And I could bite my sister for no apparent reason. Then, one day, it got pushed out of my mouth and banned forever. It was suddenly like an orphan that never had a home.

And then I start to hear musings about the Tooth Fairy. What could anyone want to do with my tooth? It was such an odd item. I guess it could be made into a cufflink. Or, a strange ornament attached to a gold chain. Maybe someone could save up a few and trade them for Green Stamps? Surely, some Grandmother would find this to be a wonderful keepsake.

I didn't really need it anymore. It was kind of small. And a funny shape. It couldn't fit back into the slot from where it came from. That's kind of true about most things that the body tosses out. So, go ahead.

Write me a check. Or leave a Money Order, or a bank transfer (but, they didn't do those kinds of things back in the late 1940s). This arrangement was my first introduction to a trade for money and I didn't want to screw it up.

You left a dollar? What would I do with a dollar? I didn't even know what money was used for. How 'bout a toy? Or some "psghetti"? That's what I called my favorite food when I was little. Maybe this dollar thing wasn't such a great deal. Maybe I should have read that book, *The Art of the Deal*. Oops .. I almost broke the rules about avoiding political commentary.

So just what is a Tooth Fairy?

"You've got your basic Tinkerbell-type Tooth Fairy with the wings, wand, a little older and whatnot. Then you have some people who think of the tooth fairy as a man, or a bunny rabbit or a mouse." One review of published children's books and popular artwork found the Tooth Fairy to also be depicted as a child with wings, a pixie, a dragon, a blue mother-figure, a flying ballerina, two little old men, a dental hygienist, a potbellied flying man smoking a cigar, a bat or, a bear." -from a study by Rosemary Wells.

The Tooth Fairy is just one of those old *methuselah* stories that seem to be carried along from culture-to-culture and generation-to-generation. Kind of like Santa Claus and the Easter Bunny.

Parents who don't want to break the chain and kids just eat up the sweet fantasy.

Now if I was a smart and savvy kid, I would have invested that dollar in a high interest-bearing account. And I would have met up with Jeff Bezos of Bill Gates to parlay the proceeds into a Tooth Fairy Class A stock.

Round Things

I like round things. Not squares, not hexagons, not even parallelograms. I never liked geometry or trigonometry...just round things. If it had to do it with a straight line, it just wasn't my thing. Well...unless the line led me to a round thing.

I dunno. Maybe it all started when I was denied the opportunity to breastfeed. Maybe it was on my first date at an indoor movie house? It's hard to say when a passion about round things goes into action.

I like knobs: Door knobs–copper, brass or wood. it doesn't matter. I like tubes–not the ends so much, but the middle where it's filled with mushy stuff. I even like TV remotes with smooth, round, ends.

I like peaches with fuzz. Grapes give me an immense amount of pleasure. Every so often I like to squeeze a tangelo. Or a nice ripe plum. A Grapefruit could be satisfying...even if it's kind of bumpy. Actually I like just about any round thing that lives in my fruit or vegetable drawer. It gives me a special pleasure that you just can't get from a hunk of cheese.

I like rubber balls that fit into the palm of my hand.

I like a nice tush and a shoulder that slopes south and...oh, do I like a puppy's tummy!

Sometimes I think I'd like to open up a store called "Round Things" with signs everywhere that read, "Please Touch."

I don't think I'm alone on this subject. I spent nine months thinking about round things inside my mother's womb. After all, everything in there is mostly round.

Round things deliver an immense amount of pleasure. You're in the world of infinity. They're truly wonderful. There's no beginning or end. Round things could be soft and spongy or hard and shiny.

If it's round and it fits into your hand you could close your eyes and follow a sweet dream that never seems to have an end.

I like round things. They spin my socks. They wag my tail. They send me over the moon.

Public Restroom Report

"I've been everywhere, man
I've been everywhere, man
Crossed the deserts bare, man
I've breathed the mountain air, man
Of travel I've had my share, man
I've been everywhere."

JOHNNY CASH

Let's face it. If you drive north or south, east or west on America's interstates you will eventually need to stop at a rest stop. For most of us, it's not really a rest stop, it's a bathroom stop. Well, actually, it's not really a bathroom stop, unless you're planning to take off your shirt or blouse and sponge bathe in front of a public sink. So it's really a place to take care of your #1 or #2 needs.

Usually, your visit requires that you park your car, walk a ways to the entrance of a building and look for the door that reads: Men or Women. I'm not exactly sure what you do if you don't fit into one of those categories, but that's another subject for someone who is better acquainted with these issues. So I'll just park that aside and move on to the matter at hand.

Once you've decided what your needs might be (#1 or #2), it's simply a matter of entering the appropriate area and as we say to our sweet puppy, "do your business." Once you finish, it's up with your drawers, up with your zippers, up with your suspenders (if you are of a certain age), and off you go to the hand washing station.

The big dilemma here is if you'll find some soap. Sometimes you'll find a soap squirter and sometimes you won't. Sometimes it's full and sometimes it's empty (or, it only has a smidge left in the bottle). If there's only a smidge in the bottle, you'll have to pump it about 10 times to hopefully, and I did say *hopefully* get a drop of liquid soap to remove anything on your hands that shouldn't be there. Once you're done you shake your hands 12 times to extract the water.

> "Why 12 times? 12 Apostles, 12 Signs, 12 Zodiac Signs, 12 months. Why 12 months? The one I like the best? It's the biggest number with one syllable."

JOE SMITH, IN TED TALK ABOUT HAND WASHING

Then there's the hand dryer. With some hand dryers, you slide your hands into the appropriate slots and a jet engine blows off the excess water. Hopefully that's all it blows off. I generally keep an eye on my hands when they are in this contraption to be sure my skin and muscles aren't pasted on the dryer wall.

That's about it. You're ready to exit the restroom. Except there's one more thing: you encounter a sign that reads: "How did we do? Please tell us how your experience was using this restroom. Text here and leave a message."

Well I thought about it. I almost saved their text info. But, then I wondered, "Exactly how much information do they want from me?" "Were the floors wet?" "Did they put up the Caution, Floor Wet" sign?" "How many CCs did I deposit?" "How did my #2 work out?" "Was the guy in the next stall responsive when I asked him if he had any toilet paper?" "Did the room smell?" And then I stopped. This shit is getting too personal. So I left. Maybe I'll be in a better frame of mind to respond next time I visit.

*"I've been to Boston, Charleston, Dayton, Louisiana
Washington, Houston, Kingston, Texarkana
Monterey, Faraday, Santa Fe, Tallapoosa
Glen Rock, Black Rock, Little Rock, Oskaloosa
Tennessee to Tennessee Chicopee, Spirit Lake
Grand Lake, Devils Lake, Crater Lake, for Pete's sake."*

JOHNNY CASH

Mailbox

I have a deep secret that I must admit. I have a one-sided love affair with an inanimate object. She's wider than she is tall. She doesn't move with the wind but she does have an arm that moves up and down. No, she's not a blow up doll. But that's not a bad guess. Actually my love affair is more like a yearning. Sometimes it's an aching. Or, maybe it's a lusting?

It happens just about every day, usually in the early afternoon. It starts as a curiosity and increases to a forceful crescendo. Just about every day.

You'd think a guy would move on to other curiosities. After all, there are a lot of fish in the sea. Except this fish is eternally-filled with surprises. So it definitely has become my cherished ritual.

Most of the time, this yearning is really not worth the effort–except for those few orgasmic moments. And then...well the urge renews itself the next day and many days thereafter.

Some of life's experiences are difficult to describe. But not this one. On a typical day, I just get up from my easy chair, slip on my shorts, and head out of the door. And then it's just a 2-minute walk to the destination of my fantasies.

When I arrive, I take my key out and insert it into the lock. No doorbell or door knock is required. I just open the door and there it is; today's mail.

In my younger days, I dreaded opening the mailbox because most of what I found were bills. But in the retirement world, it's a whole new universe. Yeah, I still get a smattering of bills but I also get an occasional birthday or anniversary card. I receive reminders to clean my gutters and my air conditioning vents. A reminder to update my undergraduate info. And to my great and wondrous surprise, I occasionally get a government check for being a good boy (that's where the orgasmic experience hits its apex and that's when I start to fantasize that this government check thing might become a daily event).

Then, there are the weekly flyers for correcting deep vein thrombosis, cataracts, liposuction, or where to get the best deal on prosthetics. You must need a wheel alignment, synthetic oil change or engine diagnosis for your car. I just can't stand the guilt of ignoring my sweet Toyota.

Pizza? You must be craving pizza. There's the best, the finest, the deep dish, the Detroit-style (who knew Detroit had any style?) It never seems to end.

End, you say? There's always a few ads for cemetery plots, tombstones, and rent-a-chapels.

I dunno. Maybe I need to start watching reruns on the "Playboy" channel. If nothing else, the curves are much better to watch than a measly mailbox.

Masked

The first time I ever saw anyone wearing a mask was my friend Robert Barondess, when he dressed up as a pirate for Halloween. I thought he was really cool. I'm guessing I was six or seven years old. I just loved his costume. He looked so strong and powerful. Around that time I started watching "The Lone Ranger." He also wore a mask. I read somewhere that someone asked, "What's with the mask?" That question never crossed my young mind.

"He wears a mask to conceal his identity as he travels throughout the West fighting for law and order." Well, that didn't exactly give me a reason why he needed to conceal his identity. I mean, how come the policemen didn't wear masks? But, again...it was pretty cool to see a TV character in the early 1950s who was hiding his face. After all, he never had to identify himself. Everyone knew he was the Lone Ranger.

Soon more masked heroes followed on TV: Batman & Robin & Batwoman, Zorro, Spiderman, The Flash, Captain America, Iron Man, Erik (Phantom of the Opera), Catwoman, Green Lantern and on and on...

Clearly, we got comfortable with TV characters wearing masks. Not that we would ever wear them in public ourselves (unless we planned to rob a bank). As it turned out most of us got comfortable with seeing masks...until a group of Middle Eastern women started appearing in Western cities wearing their burqa masks. We soon discovered that devoted Muslim women wore these face masks to honor their religions rules and rituals. Hmm...then again, to a Western eye, it seemed strange and mysterious and a little scary. Who is that person? What is she hiding? Can I trust her? Many Americans started to think of these women as an aberration. Again, to a Western eye, they seemed to segregate themselves by wearing an unfamiliar type of clothing and a mask. As time passed, we seemed to fear them less and started to accept their customs.

And, then came COVID-19. Now, everyone was required to wear a mask. Cowboys, Indians, superheroes, Muslim women, and...you and me.

All of a sudden we were masked men and women going about our daily business: walking the dog, shopping for groceries, buying pharmaceuticals and picking up take out food. Lip reading was a thing of the past. Speak up loudly and clearly. Enunciate your words: "you want one order of Moo Goo Gai Pan or, Goo Goo Gai Sam? And an order of Sichuan Shredded Pork with Garlic Sauce or Stitch Watch Pork with Salad Soup?"

What's even weirder is that we have so quickly accepted masks as our new normal. Forget about flirting, smirking, chortling or even throwing kisses. Now, it's all dependent upon your eyes. And if you choose to wear sunglasses...well, the rest of that goes out the window.

Apart from our newfound communication problem was, to me, a big plus. While waiting on a line, I no longer had to make small talk with strangers. Since I'm an introvert by nature, the mask gave me the ability to be even more anonymous in public.

I guess the next step is to customize our masks. Drawing characters that we wish to emulate. Or adding a ventriloquist's mouth that moves up and down when we talk. Maybe we need a blinking light to indicate our approval and a honking horn to indicate our disapproval. Welcome to the new world of clowns.

My Phone is Broken, My Shoes Don't Fit, and I'm Not Wearing a Bra Anymore

How's your day going so far? Are you feeling okay? Any trouble getting out of bed? Got any pains or aches? Were you able to step into your underwear without landing on your butt? Is everything in focus? Did you check the news? That's always a good way to start your day on the wrong foot.

I don't know if it's just me or if I just happen to know a bunch of people who seem to get started with a lot of creaks and bangs. So many people write songs about long, lost love or, long, lost friendships or, long, lost ways to do math. It was so easy back then. My arm hurts. I got a sore throat. My tush is a little off.

You saw your doctor. He gave you a pill. And, that was that. It didn't matter if the pill fixed anything. It was more important that he gave you his undivided attention.

And, it was so easy to reach your doctor. You picked up the phone. Dialed his number. And, his nurse set you up with an appointment. Now? You don't even have to pick up your phone. You can ask Siri to dial it for your. "Siri, call Dr. Schmeckel."

A computer answers the phone. "Hello, you've reached the offices of Drs. Putz, Schmeckel, Schtunk and Schmeggie. Or, if you're not Jewish, "You've reached Drs. Jimmy...Crack....Corn and I Don't Care. Press 1 if you need help right away. Or, if you're experiencing erection problems, press 2 if your erection problems just went away. Press 3 if you want to talk to billing because our billing department is always available."

My sister thinks her phone is always broken. And that's possible. Personally, I think it ran out of words. Or, every button looks the same to her. She doesn't get the Face ID thingy. Do I hold it close, or from across the room? Do I aim for my better side, or the side that has too many birthmarks? Do I click on the clock, the calendar, the tiny scanner or just "Tips?" And, who do I tip? It's a complicated world.

My shoes don't fit. I keep a set of sneakers in my NY apartment and in my Florida condo. Same socks. Same size. Same width. So, how come my Florida sneakers don't fit anymore? Are my toes gaining weight? I looked up a toe diet on Google but, all I found was a ke*toe* diet. Good luck with that.

From my limited sample of the world, it seems like women have a much harder time getting shoes to fit. Personally, I think they make their purchasing decisions based on style rather than size. "This pair looks great. I think I'll just crush in my toes and nobody will notice anything weird. Of course, I do make scrunchy facial moves whenever I take a step. But...these shoes do look really great."

I wonder if they make Crocs in high heels?

My bra doesn't fit. Okay, it's clear that I'm not a woman. Whew? I can't imagine having to wear a bra everyday. You take it out of the drawer and unfold it. You pop out the cups. And, then you fit the girls into it. Now comes the torture. You need to twist your arms around your back and fit the tiny hooks into the thingies. I'd imagine this takes some practice and some twisted triceps. Then, there's that thing about wearing a gizmo that wraps around your chest like a lasso. I often wonder if an ill-fitting bra is anything like an ill-fitting shoe. To tell you the truth, I don't think I'm heading this way anytime soon.

So, that's today's rant. Maybe I'll bump into you at Dr. Schmeckle's office one day. They do have their up and down days.

Mysteries of the Universe

There's no question about it. I need to lose weight. Unfortunately, I'm just not wired to activate the "get up and go" function that some people seem to be able to easily engage. I like to write. I like to eat. I like to cook. I like to Facebook and Instagram and I like to occasionally watch some TV. But, do I naturally want to go for a walk? Do some bending? Stretching? No, but maybe some kvetching. The reports I get from my doctor are clear and precise. The problem is with the medical language he uses. I have to be honest: I don't speak in that tongue.

"Your blood sugar is too high."

Wait a minute...my what? Did I spill some blood in my Raisin Bran this morning? To my knowledge (which I admit is very limited), I haven't put any sugar in my blood. And, if I did, it surely got there by taking a shortcut through my esophagus.

Okay, now he tells me that my kidney function is too high. Really? I went to pee this morning and my...function...as far as I could tell, was working on all cylinders. Where does he find this "function switch?" Is it hidden in a fat fold that I'm not familiar with? Do I really need to see what condition my condition is in? Yeah, yeah, yeah .. oh, yeah...

My hemoglobin A1c results are slightly high, and, that's consistent with a risk of diabetes, but, according to the American Diabetes Association, hemoglobin A1c represents optimal control in non-pregnant diabetic patients. Oh, well that's comforting...I think...

Okay, let's divert a bit here. Let's talk about calories. Now there's a word I can really wrap my head around. When I'm cooking I never see any indication of how many calories I need to add to eggplant parmigiana. I don't know what they look like or taste like. So how do you control your intake if you can't see a calorie?

I've read that it's important to burn calories. *Hmmm.* That's an interesting notion. Gather up all of the calories in your kitchen, put them into a small paper bag and throw them into your barbecue grill and light a fire under them. Now that seems like a logical way to lose weight. I could probably work that into my daily routine between a nap and a snooze.

On another note, I'm told that I need to eat more protein. That seemed to make some sense. So I went to the supermarket and approached the butcher in the back. I asked him if he had any fresh protein. He said he had plenty of it. I said, "Great, can I have a pile of protein to hold me over for the next six months?" He gave me a look. You know that kind of look your high school math teacher gives you when you ask him how much is *ja-gundo*? Now, if you can't see a calorie or taste a calorie, I wonder if you can smell a protein? So, I went back to the butcher. He was still adjusting his glasses from the last look he gave. I said, "do you have any proteins that I can smell?" He took a deep breath and said, "Son, have you ever been injected, inspected, detected, infected, neglected and selected?" (Alice's Restaurant, Arlo Guthrie). I was a bit overwhelmed, but I had a feeling he was onto me. So I moved over to the vegetable department. I asked the veggie man: "Do you have any fresh protein that tastes good?"

Again, I got a look. A deep breath. I have a feeling that the butcher sent him a text about me. Well, I didn't wait for an answer.

I just went onto my final question. If I was somehow successful at losing weight, could I visit my long-lost fat somewhere? After all, it must go somewhere. I asked my wife. And I got a look.

She kindly said to me, "Honey, it's just one of those mysteries of the universe."

In her next breath she said this whole essay is indicative of my issues. Whatever that means.

New and Improved

We all have a few common greetings between friends: "What's going on?" "What do you say?" "What's up?" "What's new?"

Sometimes, "what's new?" triggers an amazing response. Of course, you never really think that you're going to discover something amazing or even interesting, but it's a good opener to start a conversation.

It's not unusual for your friend to respond by saying, "not much," at which point the conversation could end but it seldom does. Because something is always new in someone's life: a milestone, a new purchase, a change in a relationship, the results of a doctor's visit, even a bump on your head. But if you want to really pursue a conversation with this person you need to do some digging. Maybe you need to ask, "What's improved?" But you'd never say that because it sounds like what previously existed wasn't so good. "Hey, you look like you lost weight."

My response, "Why, was I fat?'

In advertising we expect to hear, "what's improved?," if, for no other reason than the advertiser has competitors and he thinks he must be one step ahead of his competitors all of the time. While this may be true, he may also risk losing his customers who were already quite pleased with "what's old." Take me, for example. I bought a computer in the late 1980s. While I wasn't quite sure why I needed one in the first place, I figured I should get on the "what's new" bandwagon while it was moving forward. Being an old dog, it took me a while to graduate from my trusty IBM Selectric. But after a while I got comfortable with this computer and we became fast friends ...*until* ... I was told I needed to upgrade my programs. "What are you talking about?"

"I know how it works and it does the job just fine."

So I ignored all of the upgrade notices for quite some time, maybe five years or so. Then the Day of Reckoning arrived. "Hey, Mr. I don't need to upgrade...well, if you don't upgrade we won't back up any of your existing programs."

"You won't back up what you sold me? How exactly does that work?"

So I put off the upgrade for even longer. Then I thought, "maybe I should upgrade?"

I went through the steps and discovered I had waited too long and they didn't offer an upgrade that requires them to go back into their Dark Ages files. So, they twisted my arm to do what they wanted. I bought a "new and improved" computer. And you know what? It's a pain in the ass to learn and doesn't make my life any easier.

And, so goes my life experiences. I fell in love with a gorgonzola salad dressing. Next thing you know it's "new and improved," so I tried it. Well it was new, but hardly improved.

Remember New Coke? Coke drinkers gave it a resounding "NO!" It's certainly new but hardly improved. And, that Heinz upside down plastic bottle? Well, the new version of this old standby certainly pours better than sticking a knife into the bottle and shaking it until it spills all over your arm. But, the design? Not hardly an aesthetic improvement. It actually looks like a ketchup bottle sitting on a toilet.

Now here's one that just gets me livid: eyeglass frames. I spend an inordinate amount of time finding a frame that suits my personality. I go from one store to another and yet another and finally find the perfect frame. I order it and begin to wear it immediately. Then one day I drop my glasses and the frame cracks. I go back to the eyeglass store, "do you still have this frame in stock?"

"No. That was discontinued."

"Seriously?"

"I just bought it less than a year ago."

"I guess there weren't many people interested in a green frame."

"Okay, I get that but, didn't the manufacturer make a few extra?"

"Apparently not. Can I interest you in a red frame?"

Grrrrrr...Not being one to give up so easily, my dear wife let her fingers do the walking on Google and ... you know what? She found exactly one frame available from an individual. Even if it wasn't the same exact shade of green, it was good enough. And it was only 58 bucks! Not the ridiculous amount the retailer charges for a new frame. I'll stick with old. You can keep your "new and improved."

Does any remember the Betamax video player? A far superior player than the VHS competitor. Yet it failed miserably. It was new and improved. But consumers wanted to record their ninety minute movies on one tape. Betamax tapes would only hold a sixty minute program. So, in this case, new and improved was the clear winner but, it just didn't work out for Sony.

And, if you're really old enough...do you remember Ford's Edsel? The Titanic of automobiles. A "new and improved" marketing disaster. After ten years and a $250 Million rollout, the auto reviews said it looked like a car sucking a lemon. "New and improved?" Maybe if it was named "Josephine" it would have fared better. Poor Henry Ford's son. What a way to be remembered.

On a personal note, after 31 years of producing and directing TV spots and corporate marketing films, I became "new and improved." Today, I'm a painter. Instead of pointing my finger at an actor or a cameraman I aim it at an easel. It's my new way of seeing the world. And, while it's new to me, I'm not sure if I'm "improved." But, I'm getting there.

Noah Zark

I can't exactly say I remember when he first walked into our lives. But I do remember it only took about three seconds to realize this puppy was meant to be part of our family. I'm guessing someone brought him to us. Or we found him in a Christmas box at a shopping mall. The details are foggy. It was 1972 or 1973. We lived on Staten Island about a mile from the Staten Island Ferry Terminal. It was a two-family house just across from a gypsum factory. As long as you kept the windows closed, it was a lovely neighborhood.

The puppy was about 3 lbs. soaking wet. A Jack Russell. Cute beyond words, spunky, playful, funny and adorable. He stole your heart the minute you met him. We named him Noah. Our funny friend Andrea said he needed a last name. So we re-named him Noah Zark.

At the time he joined our family we both had pretty busy lives. I had a full time job at an arts council and Mary Anne was working nights as a registered nurse. His first few months with us were fun. He loved to play and loved to be with us. But as he grew, he demonstrated his need to chew. Noah had an insatiable need to chew, so the destruction began. First it was the corner of a door. And then it was any pair of shoes he could find. And then it was Mary Anne's favorite expensive Italian shoes. Then it was the couch. It would have been smart if we bought him a bag of bones. But the thought never crossed our minds.

Yet, something needed to change or the entire contents of our apartment could have been sold as stuffing for a stuffed animal factory. So I decided he needed to go out, on his own, to burn off some of that puppy energy. Once I decided this was the plan, I took Noah outside and let him go. A few hours later he returned. A little dirty, a little tired, but happy to have a place to sleep and a meal to eat. So, I tried it again. And again, he returned in the same condition as the first time out. I don't know how many days this scenario went on but it seemed to work for everyone's needs.

Except one day I came home from work and Noah was not to be found. I looked up and down the block and around the corner. I drove around the neighborhood calling out his name. No response. So I went home hoping he would show up sometime later. And, the phone rang about 5:30 PM. "Hello"

"Hello, do you own a dog named Noah Zark?'

"Yes, I do."

"Well this is the Manager at the Staten Island Ferry. I have him in my office. We found him on the boat as it was about to leave the dock."

"Oh, man. Thank you. I'll be over there in a jiffy."

When I came by to pick him up he was happy as a clam (as happy as a clam *can* be).

So, come morning – the old routine began anew. And off Noah went to wherever made him happy. Dogs, as I was later to learn, are creatures of habits. If they find a place to play, they return to the scene of the crime. Little did I know that Noah soon returned to the auto loading platform of the Staten Island Ferry. Apparently, the gates closed, and off it went onto the big city called Manhattan Island.

I returned from work that day. And again, Noah was nowhere to be found. And again, I looked all over the neighborhood. And again, I returned home and the phone rang, "Hello?"

"Yes, Hello."

"Do you have a dog named Noah Zark?"

"Yes, I do."

"Well, I have him."

"Can you tell me where you are and I'll come by to pick him up?"

(long pause)

"I'm on Broad St."

"Oh, well I can be there in about 10 minutes. I work near there on Staten Island."

(long pause)

"Uh, mister .. I have your dog on Broad Street near Wall Street in Manhattan."

I breathe deep and say to myself: "I can't believe that stupid dog took a ride on the ferry."

"Oh, man .. you are so kind. I'll jump in my van and meet you there as soon as I can get there." As I recall, it was about a 45 minute ride at full speed. And there they were, a businessman in a suit and Noah Zark looking tired and haggard. "Thank you so much. What do I owe you?"

'I bought him two hot dogs. You owe me 50 cents."

Clearly, the man really wanted to take Noah home with him but felt a responsibility to return him to his rightful owner. I thanked him and off we went from Manhattan over the Brooklyn Bridge to the Gowanus Expressway and over the Verrazano Bridge. Whew! What an adventure.

A day or two later I let him out again. Sadly, this time he ran out of luck. He was hit by a car and went to a place where doggies play forever. It was a very sad day for a very sweet-spirited doggie. Rest In Peace, Noah Zark. I hope to see you again someday. Maybe we can ride the ferry together and visit Chinatown or Little Italy. I hear the food is better in that part of town.

Storage

When you're retired you have a lot of time on your hands.

"Sometimes I sits and thinks and, sometimes I just sits."

SATCHEL PAIGE

That's actually a pretty good quote because it kind of sums up my retired life. Of course, when I "thinks," that's when I kind of go off the rails. I think of what is and what could be. I think of what I should do and what I'm actually doing. I think about which store I should go to for our grocery shopping, oh, this list goes on and on…"this store has a bunch of 2-for-ones," "this store has cream cheese,"–bless their souls, "this store has shitty bagels," (shame shame on them). The mind is a terrible thing to waste.

Sometimes I think I could be a great songwriter. Like these couple of lines:

"I don't want to set the world on fire. I just want to set a flame in your heart."

THE INKSPOTS

Sometimes–for no particular reason–I just sits and thinks about stuff I'd like to know more about–like a woman's pocketbook. It's really an amazing contraption. It doesn't matter if it's a shoulder bag, handbag or purse. In reality it's just a portable storage container.

So what's in it?

Ah, let's cut to the chase. It's got keys and keys. More keys than you could possibly know what they open. And glasses: regular glasses, sunglasses and reading glasses, because you never know... It's got tissues and band-aids and medicines: medicines for your tummy, your headaches, earaches and muscle aches. And make up—you just have to have make up. Blush and lipstick and eye liner and a nail cutter and nail file. And eye shadow and eye shadow remover. And lipstick remover. And nail color remover. Because the night is young and you might want to change your mood. It's got an elegant night watch that you can't read and a day watch with numbers so large that they can't fit in your pocketbook. There's a checkbook and a cell phone and a few ball point pens that always seem to be dry. Then there are writing pads with lists. To-do lists, to-don't lists, to-remember lists, and lists of restaurants and reviews. Receipts from CVS. Well, I wouldn't really call them receipts. They're more like a *tallit* (a prayer shawl for religious Jews). A typical CVS receipt can be wrapped around your shoulders and touch both sides of the ground. Sometimes there's even a can of repellent for bugs and one for those who bug you.

Why does it have so many zippers?

It's like a file cabinet. Medicines here, keys there, phone here, but, here's the funny thing—when the phone rings, good luck finding the right compartment!

Why are the contents such a secret?

Why can a man get away with only carrying his phone, keys and wallet (and, maybe a handkerchief) and a woman has to carry a loaded potato? Do women really need to carry butter, sour cream, a roll or tin foil, and the entire microwave oven?

The pocketbook. The mystery of mysteries. Don't leave home without it.

Visiting Doctors

In the past couple of weeks, I've had the distinct pleasure of visiting a few doctors. Well actually five of them. One led to another and another and another.

Originally, I thought I had a polyp on my vocal cord. So I found a doc on Google. Yeah, that's the new way to find a doc. The old way being that you ask a friend who asks a friend. Their opinion is usually based upon some peripheral observation: "I liked him," "He was kind," "He asked me about my sebaceous cyst," (I'm only kidding. Somehow this ailment always makes me laugh).

Okay, I found the Ear, Nose and Wallet Doctor (that's David Letterman's description). I called her office and then it began, "welcome to the Blah Blah Blah Offices of Drs. Lip, Dr. Sponge, and Dr. Pepper."

"Press 1 if you know the person's extension. And, if you don't know the person's extension, why are you calling us? Press 2 if you know where we are located. Press 3 if you speak Ashkenazi."

Okay, I called for an appointment, "Do you have, have you had, do you expect to have, do you know anybody who has had COVID-19? How 'bout COVID-18? COVID-17? Do you have a cough? Has anybody put his fingers under your private area and asked you to cough? Where have you been in the last 24 hours? Did you have fun?"

"Okay, we have an available appointment in August 2024. What time would you like to come in?"

Okay, so I finally got an appointment and visited the doctor, "Let's take a look at your throat. Open wide. I'm just going to stick this long metal rod with a flashlight and a video camera to see what's doing down there."

"Oh, yeah. You have a polyp on your vocal cord."

Duh. I didn't go to medical school and I could have made this diagnosis.

"And, it looks like you have some thingy below your vocal cord that looks like it's been irritated. How are you feeling otherwise?"

"Well, I've been a little off balance lately and my neck is kind of stiff."

"*OHHHHHH*, well, let's not do anything until we find out about what's going on with you. You'll need to see a Family Practice Doc, a Neurologist, a Physical Medicine Doc, and a Gastroenterologist."

The party begins. You'll need an MRI of your head, an MRI of your back, a back x-ray, a needle test to check the nerves in your legs, and an endoscopy. And of course, we'll need to take a gallon of your blood. All of this because I have a polyp in my throat.

All of this has been quite an adventure. If you've never had an MRI, beware. It's like being buried alive with a bevy of heavy duty cymbals and clangs. "How long will this take?" "Oh about 15 minutes." Ladies and gentlemen, trust me when I tell you, this will be the longest 15 minutes of your life. It will feel like your life is coming to an end. And, just when you're ready to give in, the MRI machine will crank up and slide you out of your living hell.

Well, all of the procedures are over and I'm waiting for my follow up appointments to hear the results and prognosis. But first–would you kindly respond to our survey? "How did we do? Did we treat you like a king? Did we listen to all of your kvetching? Was the nurse the kindest person you ever met? Did the doctor make you feel extra special? Did you get a hug when you left? (Oh, wait, it's COVID-time .. no hugs).

The neck pain was fixed with a cortisone shot. Everything else remains the same. That throat thingy is still there.

31 Years in the Film Business

For some odd reason, I chose to spend most of my career in the film business. I started off with a partner and we produced TV spots. We got lucky at the onset and landed a job from J. Walter Thompson. They had a new client who owned a radio station in Washington, DC. And they had a new disc jockey–Howard Stern. Since Howard was an early "shock jock" DJ, it wasn't too hard to find stories to tell about this radio character. But, the trick was to be able to tell them in 10-second commercials.

One spot featured young Howard in Elementary School, another as if he was admitted to a Psych Ward in a hospital...

They were all sight gags and one was funnier than the other.

I remember going to the casting session to interview actors. It was 1981. We had just started our business. I couldn't stop laughing all day. And that's when I said to myself, "this is a really funny way to make a living."

That package of spots set us off on a path of being known as the guys who produce funny TV spots. So we followed *this* job with spots for Hop-In Stores, DC Lottery, Pimlico Race Track, The Washington Times, Northern Neck Ginger Ale, EZ Roller Paint Brushes, Cub Cadet Lawn Tractors, and on and on. One job was funnier than the next.

One time we were filming a spot for Stihl Chainsaws. We were up in the Cascade Mountains planning to cut down a redwood tree with a consumer chainsaw (we actually had to bring a notary public with us to prove this was possible). Once we drove up to the location from Seattle, we had a bit of a hike in front of us. And the hiking required us to climb over some seriously wide trees that were already cut down, blocking the pathway. As we climbed over the 2nd or 3rd cut tree, one of our crew members said, "If I knew about this hike in advance I would have quoted you for our Sherpa Services."

In order to capture the tree falling down, we set up three cameras. I was operating the third camera. Before we start rolling, the professional logger tells us that once these tall trees hit the ground, an occasional branch will go flying at a very high rate of speed in any direction.

"So be careful."

We start rolling. The tree fell. I was situated low to the ground. And just as he said, a branch came whizzing by about 50 feet from our location. Oh boy, that was scary.

The TV spots led to longer format films for meetings and public relations for clients such as CSX Corporation, The Greenbrier Hotel, The NutraSweet Company, and recruitment videos for private schools and colleges.

It was, indeed, a fun way to make a living.

Is That All There Is?

So you want a vaccine shot, eh? Well, first you have to "call this number." What number? Oh, you'll have to look on the internet. Or watch local TV news. Then when you find the "number" you dial it up. Ring, ring, ring, ring...finally, a voice answers: "if you're calling to set up an appointment to get a vaccine shot you're shit out of luck. All slots have been assigned. Try calling back another time. You might be able to set up an appointment in 3012."

So you call again. Nobody picks up the phone. You find another number to call, "sorry, all slots have been assigned and we have no idea when the feds will resupply the vaccine. Call again."

Two weeks later Mary Anne calls again, to a number in Fort Lauderdale. And someone actually answers the phone. She gets an appointment and then asks about me: "No, we can't give 'him' a shot. Just the caller."

"WHAT??? What do you mean?? He's my husband!"

"Congratulations. What's his e-mail address?"

"theotherdonald@gmail.com."

"You're kidding me, right?"

An hour later we get an email to fill out a form, print it, and bring it to the Hard Rock Stadium on the assigned date and time. "And, don't come early!" The time comes to head to the Hard Rock and we decide to leave a bit early just in case there's traffic or an accident or something. Uh, oh...we're 45 minutes early. Maybe we can find a place to get a cup of coffee? Are you kidding?? There isn't a joint within 20 miles of this place to get a cup of coffee. So, we drive around...aimlessly...for a while.

And then we head back to the entrance where you're supposed to get on line to get a shot.

First we see a slew of police cars. Maybe 30 of them. All spread out like they were expecting an insurgency. We stop to talk to one of the cops. He looks at my wife and says, "you can't get a vaccine. You look way too young." A refreshing wiseguy comment. We proceed. The next guy we encounter asks to see the form we filled out. He glances at it and writes some squiggle on our windshield. We proceed. The next guy asks us for our driver's license. He looks at them and writes another squiggle on our windshield. He says to proceed. The third woman we encounter asks to see the form we filled out and printed at home. She asks me to hold it up to the window and she proceeds to copy it word for word. Then she asks me to sign it with my pen, but I can't touch the paper. Did you try to do that? It's not possible to write your signature that resembles your signature. Why would she ask us to re-do what we already did? She's told without touching the paper. And, why do we need to do it this way? "It might contain the virus."

She finishes and again writes some squiggle on the windshield. Now we definitely can't see shit out the front window.

Next, we get our car on line. Originally, we were told it would only take 15 minutes. Well, we're on line for two hours. Inching along....two inches at a time. Then we are asked to open our window just a crack, "do you have an appointment?"

Are you fucking kidding me? I went through this insane process and got to you and you're just getting around to asking me if I have an appointment?? "Yeah, we have an appointment."

"Okay, proceed forward".

Finally, we reach the tent where they are administering the shot. "Now, they do the Arlo Guthrie "Alice's Restaurant" song routine: Have you been " injected, inspected, detected, infected, neglected, and selected?" Have you been here or there, near or far, touched much by anyone wherever, whatever or whenever? Are you allergic to this or that, such and such or have you ever now or then? "Well, I was once ..."

"Nevermind that, just roll up your sleeve. One, two...there you go. Now you're done. Pull ahead and wait in your car for 30 minutes."

"Is there a bathroom? I've been in the car since yesterday."

"Yes, there's a port-a-potty that says 'Doodie Calls' on the door."

Oh, that's lovely.

Thirty minutes pass, and off we go only to return to this bureaucratic insanity in three weeks.

Says my wife, "You're way too negative."

"You think so? Hey, I'm from New York. And, by the way, it's 'on line,' not 'in line.'"

> *"And when I was twelve years old*
> *My daddy took me to the circus, the greatest show on Earth*
> *There were clowns and elephants and dancing bears*
> *And a beautiful lady in pink tights flew high above our heads*
> *And as I sat there watching*
> *I had the feeling that something was missing*
> *I don't know what, but when it was over I said to myself*
> *Is that all There Is?"*

"IS THAT ALL THERE IS?" SUNG BY PEGGY LEE

It's All Gone

There are no clams in my clam chowder.
There's no coffee in my sac.
The Parmesan Cheese disappeared in a sneeze.
There's no gray paint left in the can.
Or any toothpaste in the tube.
My closet is full with a bunch of my clothes, but they don't fit over my tummy.
I'm all out of underwear but that's no surprise.
Hellman's went bad last week.
The Lactaid went south and the spinach is weeping.
Heinz has left town.
And so has Dijon.
What's a decent hot dog to do today?
The seltzer is flat. The ice cream went splat. And the fork ran away with the spoon.
Now it looks like my pen is almost out of ink. And this is my last sheet.
Don't you think it's about time for a sexy tomato to come my way? Or, even a kumquat would do.
There must be love somewhere out there .
Or, maybe not now, you know.
The postman did leave a note. I think it was a love letter but it wasn't addressed to me.
I know this sounds like a suicide note but, to be truthful I just have to pee.

Just Yesterday

Just yesterday life was sweet. Everything seemed to work the way you expected it to be. You woke up and brushed your teeth. The toothpaste tasted just as expected. You turned on the shower faucet and…eventually…hopefully…you got hot water. You prepared your coffee, pressed a few buttons and it started to brew. The toaster toasted, the refrigerator chilled, the frying pan got hot, the butter melted, the eggshells cracked, the eggs cooked… it all worked as expected.

You trusted that it would all work. You trusted that you wouldn't get sick or be poisoned by each and every thing you put into your mouth each and everyday.

You trusted that your car would work–safely. And that everyone around you understood the rules of the road. That red means stop and green means go. And when you parked your car at the supermarket it would be exactly where you left it in the parking lot.

You trusted that the air you breathe would be clean and clear of any dangers. And then it happened. Just like that (snaps fingers).

Put on a mask. Rub this stuff on your hands. Put on gloves. Stay at least six feet apart. Don't go swimming in the pool. Don't sit on the park bench. Don't trust anyone! Because if you do, they could kill you.

In just an instance, yesterday changed everything.

You can't go to work. You can't go out to play. You can't go to the park. You can't fly on an airplane. You can't drive into another city without being quarantined for fourteen days. You can't visit your loved ones. And even if you could, you can't kiss or hug them.

This instant change didn't just happen to you or to your son or to his boss or to your old friend. It happened to everyone all over your city, state, country–from New York to California. It happened in Italy and China. The whole world changed just like that (snaps fingers).

Trust went flying out the window...just yesterday.

Will we ever be able to trust anyone ever again? Or is this the new normal for the world?

"Yesterday, all my sorrows seemed so far away. Oh, I believe in yesterday...."

KuKuLitz

My sister passed away last week. Yes, it was sad. 81 years old. Married 61 years. Two kids. Four grandkids. A brother. Some nephews. And a few older first cousins...some in their early to mid-90s.

Most would describe her life as pretty standard "middle class." Be a wife, a mother, a grandmother... Stay in touch with high school friends. Play cards. Change diapers. Laugh. Go for walks and argue (that was kind of standard operating procedure between my sister and brother-in-law).

Although she didn't have much interest in debate on subjects beyond the scope of her home, she was generally happy with an occasional trip to Hawaii. All-in-all she was appreciated and loved.

Except for the past six months (when dementia took its toll), she spent most of her time in her Florida apartment reading, watching TV, and being cared for by two very competent nurse's aides.

I can't say I knew my sister very well. We didn't play together very much when we were young. And when she turned twenty, (I was fifteen) she got married. A few years later, I got drafted into the Army. And after 22 months and 10 days I got out and joined the hippie community. That step was a far cry from my sister's middle class world. We did see each other every so often over the next so many years. But it was always with the families, kids, holidays, etc. I can't remember a conversation we ever had that covered a newspaper story.

I shared the sad news of my sister's passing with my oldest cousin. She's fourteen years older than me. My dad lived with her family until he got married around age 40. So you could say she knew another side of my father that never crossed my path.

We reminisced. My dad was a partner in an apron manufacturing company with his three other brothers. One of them was my dad's oldest brother. I think my dad lived in my cousin's bedroom (by himself).

During our last phone chit-chat my cousin recalled that my sister had an invisible friend named KuKuLitz. This was the first time I ever heard about this invisible friend. Apparently, this friendship made my mother crazy. Who knows where it came from and who knows why? It certainly piqued my curiosity.

My parents were not what you would call "wise guys." Everything was pretty much straight-and-narrow. Except, my dad, who was an orphan at an early age, always had a nickname for some oddball character in a conversation: "Hi dad, did anybody call?"

"Yeah," he replied.

"Chaim Schmeril and *Hai Dos a Ha Fotz."*

So maybe it's possible she got this KuKuLitz thing from my father? Or maybe she got it from my crazy Uncle Jack. He was one of my mother's oldest brothers. And, he was always funny and a wise guy.

Or maybe my sister had a wild imagination. And this invisible character carried her through some tough childhood dreams.

So who was KuKuLitz? There was a TV show back then called "Kukla Fran and Ollie." The show first aired in 1947. That's the year I was born. I did some internet research and this is where it brought me:

"It was a puppet show that included Kukla, the earnest leader of the troupe, Ollie, a roguish dragon, Madame Oglepuss, a retired opera diva, Beulah Witch, a brash, madcap witch, Fletcher Rabbit, the troupe's mailman and resident fussbucket who in keeping with the show's. Unrestrained use of puns, also worked at "The Egg Plant", Cecil Bill, the troupe's union stagehand who spoke in unintelligible "tooie talk", Colonel Crackie, a Southern Gentleman, Dolores Dragon, Ollie's younger cousin, and a number of others." (Wikipedia)

So, maybe, just maybe, my sister identified with Kukla? Or, better yet, Cecil Bill who spoke "unintelligible 'tooie talk'"? Oh would I like to know the truth about this hidden secret! Since I love to talk in gibberish to an old friend who lives in Jerusalem, we could have opened a whole new world out there for kids who needed a relief from their parents.

Sadly, we'll never know. Except for my 93 year old cousin. She still laughs remembering these times.

The Me Nobody Knows

"Are you talking to me? Are YOU talking to me? ARE YOU talking to me? You better be talking to me ... well, I'm the only one here. You better be talking to me."

ROBERT DENIRO, TAXI DRIVER

Do you remember when you were still in-vitro? Oh come on...you remember when your sister pulled the fire alarm on the street corner. And, the loud alarm sounded. Your mother and father grabbed both of you and ran like hell. Oh boy, you sure do remember that bumpity bumpity run your mother did.

You don't remember me, do you? I was the toddler who opened the door under the kitchen sink, grabbed the huge container of flour, judiciously opened the screw top and dumped it all onto the floor. I was so proud of myself... until I got a *pach* in *tookus*.

I was the 5-year old in the Bronx park who thought it would be fun to take the slide down going head first. It was fun until I broke my nose. Do you remember riding with me in the police car to the hospital?

Do you remember the 6-year old who decided he didn't need to hold his mother's hand when he crossed the big street with cars whizzing by. Oh boy, that was a big metal bumper that sent him flying high in the air.

Do you remember when my sister yelled to our mother, "Is he dead?"

"Nah," the doctor said. He's just got a bunch of scrapes on his knees and forehead. He looks like a clown.

Do you remember when I got drunk at our family's Passover dinner in 1957? That Manischewitz Grape Wine went down so smoothly. About as fast as he fell asleep on the floor in the dining room.

Do you remember when I was 15 and stole my parent's car? I called my friend, Michael Axelrod. He was the neighborhood king of all things bad. I drove around the block and the car stalled. Do you remember that I told you my heart was beating about a thousand miles a minute. That I was hoping... praying...that Axelrod could get the car running again and return home before my parents realized what happened. Alexrod...now, there was a name that was filled with irony.

Do you remember after all of those shenanigans, the thing you liked most about me was that I liked to make people laugh? You just loved my jokes, right? Even if they were dumb. Do you remember that I once heard a comedian say that if a joke made ME laugh it was a good joke. Even if nobody else understood it. It was like an inside pitch. A surprise .. that was the essence of a good joke.

I'm not sure when I turned the corner on being funny. Maybe it was when I discovered girls. They liked to laugh. And, it didn't take me too long to realize that if you made them laugh they became interested in me. I'd say something funny and they would laugh. I would say something crazy and they would laugh. And, the next thing you know, well, that's when it got a little weird for me because I was scared of girls. Thank God for that surge of testosterone.

And then it clicked. Do you remember when I seemed to find just about everything funny. I was a conversational comedian. If someone said something boring, I found a reason to make it funny. Do you remember when a conversation turned bleak ...when someone had to do one better when someone was talking about death or imminent death. I would instantly change the subject with, "Did you hear what Howard Stern said yesterday? "

Everyone would stop in their tracks and I would laugh and laugh. I always seemed to turn the conversation into a laugh. Do you think

I can remember any of the funny situations? No. Do you think I can remember any of the funny jokes? No. But, you do remember that I made you laugh, right? Do you remember that they were the best of times? Indeed.

Do you remember me now? I'm the guy who loves to laugh.

www.ingramcontent.com/pod-product-compliance
Lightning Source LLC
Chambersburg PA
CBHW070547010526
44118CB00012B/1249